Sunset

ORIENTAL COOK BOOK

By the Editors of Sunset Books
and Sunset Magazine

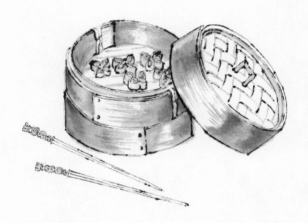

LANE BOOKS • MENLO PARK, CALIFORNIA

CHOPSTICK COOKERY FOR BEGINNERS

Although anyone who has already cooked Oriental food will find it useful, this book is designed to give beginners all the help and encouragement needed.

The recipes themselves give you the most help. They are clearly written, omit no details, and have been thoroughly tested. Any special cooking techniques (and these are few) are thoroughly described.

But beginners at Oriental cooking need even more help than a good recipe. One barrier to beginning is getting to know the infinite variety of Oriental ingredients available. The majority of recipes here do not require ingredients that require a trip to a special store. But some do gently introduce you to readily-liked exotic foodstuffs. Every special ingredient item in a recipe includes a page-number reference to the Ingredient Shopping Guide chapter. There you will find a description of the ingredient, information about how it is labeled or packaged, pronunciation of its Chinese or Japanese name (or both), and a general guide to what kind of stores sell it.

Much other help is given. The opening chapter, The Essence of an Oriental Art, distills very simple principles that apply to Chinese, Japanese, and Korean cooking alike. You will quickly learn the few important things you must do to make your first Oriental dishes turn out just right.

You are given much information in another chapter about special cooking utensils, tools, and serving dishes that are fun to own. But, to encourage you to begin, it is firmly pointed out that *no special equipment* is required. You can prepare nearly every recipe without buying a single item.

EDITED by Marjorie Ray Piper

ILLUSTRATIONS by Dinah James.

COVER PHOTOGRAPH by Glenn Christiansen. Menus and dish featured: Chinese "Hot Pot" Dinner, pages 27 and 58.

PHOTOGRAPHERS: Clyde Childress—page 49. Glenn Christiansen—cover, pages 28 (top right), 31 (bottom), 61, 77, 78, 82. Blair Stapp—pages 18, 36 (bottom left). Darrow M. Watt—pages 10, 13, 15, 28 (top left, bottom left, bottom right), 31 (top), 36 (top, bottom right), 41, 45, 46, 52, 56, 59, 64, 67, 70, 72, 85, 93.

Fourth Printing November 1971
All rights reserved throughout the world.
First Edition. Copyright © 1970 by Lane Magazine & Book Company, Menlo Park, California.
Library of Congress No: 78-100903.
SBN Title No: 376-02531-X.
Lithographed in U.S.A.

CONTENTS

THE ESSENCE OF AN ORIENTAL ART

Simple principles to help you cook authentic dishes

Most cooks in Western countries have always regarded the preparation of Chinese, Japanese, and Korean foods as the inscrutable Oriental cookery. Mysterious. Enigmatic. And difficult to understand. How sadly wrong.

What goes on behind the bamboo kitchen curtain is logical, reasonable, and as simple as a bowl of rice.

The people of these old cultures have spent hundreds of years studying what makes food good. Throughout this time, they have even developed a philosophy about food and aesthetic standards. Very little about their cooking is accidental.

Good Oriental cooks think. They choose their ingredients, cut them, and assemble them according to a plan.

They know many time-tested little ways of judging quality. They use their eyes, nose, fingers, and even their ears to judge whether the food is cooking just the right way.

They may even know about the history of the dishes they prepare or legends about how these dishes were invented. They are concerned about the healthfulness of the food, its medicinal properties, and perhaps even its religious significance.

This does not mean that you must go through a complicated course of study to prepare Oriental food well. Quite the opposite. It means that pointers, principles, and tips have already been worked out to guide you so you don't have to learn by trial and error. Of all the cuisines of the world, the Oriental are probably the most scrutable.

The following pages will try to distill the essence of what makes Oriental cooking Oriental. You will quickly get an idea of the few important necessities for success. For Oriental cooking is very different from the American school of hate-to-cook, can-opener casseroles. Instead of piling a lot of ingredients together and hoping for the best, you assemble them with a tested plan that will *guarantee* you the best.

The only difficult part of such cooking for an American is learning about ingredients which are completely strange—often labelled with Oriental characters or under a variety of names or barely labelled at all. This book contains an extensive guide to ingredients which should help you tremendously.

Nevertheless, you don't need to become an expert on the unusual foods to begin cooking. Most of the recipes here use few, if any, special ingredients (*very* few that require a trip to an Oriental market).

Yet some of the recipes do gently introduce you to new cooking materials, especially those you may like easily.

The most helpful aspect of this book is the recipes themselves. They tell you in great detail, step by step, exactly what to do. Often they warn you of mistakes to avoid.

If you do no more than merely follow the recipes in this book as you would any recipe, you will eat well the Oriental way.

SELECT THE FRESHEST & BEST INGREDIENTS

Almost any Oriental cook book you pick up will contain many pages about how to select the very best and freshest ingredients.

This fact alone proves just how logical the preparation of Oriental food is. It is perfectly logical that you must begin with the best to end with the best.

Quality ingredients are essential to delicious dishes anywhere in the world. But quality is more important for Oriental dishes for a number of reasons. First, many foods are not cooked very long—tough meat does not have time to tenderize and old vegetables do not have time to soften or change form. Such cooking merely "marries" the ingredients. It doesn't change them. One purpose of this brief cooking is to *feature* the quality of the ingredients.

Additionally, there are few sauces which mask flavor or appearance. Most of the sauces are designed to enhance, not disguise.

When you eat with a fork, you often pick up several different ingredients at the same time. But when you eat with chopsticks, you pick up just one morsel alone—one green pea, one shrimp, one slice of carrot. And as you pick it up, most of whatever sauce is coating it drops off. Chopsticks lift every small bite up to the close scrutiny of eye and tongue.

If you sneak an oversized, limp, and aged green pepper into spaghetti sauce, most people will probably never know it. But use that pepper in a Chinese vegetable dish where you cut it in squares and cook it just a minute or two, and you'll pay the piper. That pepper will spoil the dish. It will look sickly, be flabby, and taste bitter.

You needn't make a fetish of freshness. And you needn't spend half a day going to special markets, choosing your chickens still cackling, and picking your own vegetables. Just be discriminating. Don't buy what isn't good.

Learn to look for signs of freshness in vegetables. Pick out the best, or ask if more is in the storeroom.

When it comes to seafood, you need to be particularly careful about what you buy. Now it is practically impossible to get shrimp, scallops, or lobster which have not been frozen. At least be sure the frozen product is solidly frozen and bears no sign of having been partially thawed and refrozen (pools of frozen juices) or having been frozen too long (a certain grayish look). You probably can find fresh crab, oysters, and clams—which don't take freezing as well as the firmer shellfish.

Buy fish which has never been frozen if possible, although this is becoming increasingly difficult. Learn to look a fresh fish in the eye and gills. The eyes should be firm, clear, and bright. The gills should be reddish inside. A whole fish should look firm with no trace of sliminess, whether fresh or frozen and thawed. Whenever fish has been cut, the pieces should be moist and lively in color—fresh-looking.

A native-born Oriental cook will undoubtedly have higher standards of freshness than you want or can find. Someone who is used to selecting chickens and fish which are still alive can never quite adjust to what is available under the American marketing system. Such a person finds most freezing unacceptable.

But freezing does not affect all foods alike. Some, such as red meats and poultry, are not as much affected as some fish is. Some frozen vegetables may have been picked younger and may be of more dependable quality than the fresh ones available during most seasons. In some areas, the only edible-pod peas you may find will be frozen ones. Even the most finicky Oriental cooks have learned that partially frozen meat is much easier to cut in the neat, thin slices necessary for so many dishes.

Another tip about getting the best quality is this: Try to take advantage of the vegetables and fruits which are at the peak of their season. These have fuller flavor, more natural vine-ripened color, and firmer texture if cooked.

You may find it more satisfactory to plan your menus, at least partially, at the market. If you find some particularly choice-looking foods, include a dish featuring them.

You needn't make a fetish of freshness and quality. But if you want to think as an Oriental cook does and want dishes with an authentic look and flavor, you will consider freshness and quality when you shop. You will also cook perishable things as soon as possible and serve them immediately.

CUT, SLICE & ARRANGE THE FOOD CAREFULLY

If there is any one aspect that distinguishes Oriental cooking from all others and unites the differences between Chinese, Japanese, and Korean, it is the attention given to cutting food before it is cooked or assembled.

Slicing, dicing, mincing, chopping, slivering, and sectioning all are techniques employed for cooking anywhere.

But in the Orient, these ways of cutting food assume unusual importance. You can have all the proper ingredients and prepare them just as instructed; but if you don't cut those ingredients properly, the dish won't look right and won't taste right.

In fact, you may not even be able to eat the dish with chopsticks. For unless a food is soft and can be torn into small bits or is clinging enough to be scooped on top of the sticks, you must pick the food up with a pincers-like motion. Anything very large simply cannot be picked up this way. So most firm foods are cut in pieces small enough to be picked up and put into the mouth whole.

The cutting of foods also is extremely important for appearance. You'll notice how neatly everything is cut. If something is cut in cubes, these cubes are all about the same size and really cubes—not lop-sided geometric monstrosities. If something is sliced, the slices are all about the same thickness and the sliced pieces are all about the same size.

This uniformity may be carried still further. A good illustration is the familiar Chinese dish of Sweet-and-Sour Shrimp, which contains whole shrimp, green pepper, onion, and perhaps carrots, tomatoes, or pineapple. Each ingredient will be cut in pieces of similar size, and the pieces of everything will *all* be about the same size, the size of the whole shrimp. Just imagine how this dish would look if the green pepper were cut in chunks, the onions in rings, the carrots in strips, the tomatoes in thin wedges, and the pineapple in dice.

This hodgepodge wouldn't even look Chinese.

It also wouldn't taste right, not just because of its appearance but because some of the ingredients would be overcooked and some undercooked. For, in this very reasonable cuisine, ingredients are cut uniformly so that they will *cook* uniformly.

Once you begin thinking of examples of Oriental dishes, you will be amazed at how important cutting is. The neat slicing is as much a part of the dish as the food itself.

Oriental cooks regard cutting as more important than cooking. They slave over the chopping block more than over the hot stove.

You don't have to acquire an arsenal of special knives, however. A good French knife or other knife with wedge-shaped blade, or even a small cleaver, works well for almost everything.

All you must do is cut the food as the recipe tells you, but carefully.

LET THE FOOD ITSELF BE BEAUTIFUL

Most Oriental food looks marvelous. It is obvious that cooks take great pains to please all the senses.

Yet when you consider just what makes these dishes look so appealing, you become aware that garnish and elegant utensils are not the secret. The food itself is beautiful.

The beauty may be in the clarity and sparkle of a sauce or soup. Sometimes it is in the shape of the food—carefully cut and arranged slices, the simple honesty of a whole fish resting in one piece on a platter, or in the clever way dough is folded.

Color makes a main contribution. It may be obvious in the brilliant contrasting colors of a mixed vegetable dish, or more subtle in the glazed, browned skin of a duck.

The beauty may be in texture, whether it be the crisp fried coating on a pink shrimp or the baby-smooth skin of a steamed bun.

Sometimes the appeal is in action or sound—of red beef strips hitting a hot pan with a sizzle or the communal "hot pot" simmering and steaming. Other times the appeal is still-life-like. A few choice foods have been arranged so harmoniously they defy being disturbed, much less swallowed.

As you use the recipes in this book, many aesthetic qualities will automatically be cooked into the dishes you prepare.

Garnish is used with restraint and thought. Seldom will you see such massive embellishments as the scrolls of mashed potatoes, beds of chopped aspic, or masses of parsley typical of European high cuisine. Seldom, too, will you see something as unimaginative as the sprig of parsley on a blue-plate special. The garnish is more likely to be a single maple leaf, a pink-tipped ginger sprout, a dusting of toasted sesame seed, or a sprinkling of vari-colored pickle slivers.

The main beauty should be in the food itself

with the garnish being strictly according to the dictionary: "embellishment; ornament; a savory and unusually decorative condiment." Most Oriental garnishes are more than just embellishment. They are savory condiments which are an essential part of the dish. The recipes will include these, of course.

Because the beauty is in the food, simplicity is typical of its presentation. Authentic dishes and other table accessories are not essential. Several different kinds of dishes you already have may serve well. All-white or solid-colored dishes are suitable. Much very ornate fine china has a definite Oriental look (some of the designs have even been copied from old porcelain). Modern rustic or pottery table settings may be very much like Japanese pottery, or made in Japan.

In serving, just consider these small but important tips: Arrange the food in an orderly fashion and don't put too much food on the serving dishes. Platters heaped high and bowls filled to the rim somehow don't look Oriental. Plenty of the dish should be showing. In serving Japanese food, it is especially important to be skimpy and neat with servings or portions.

In the Orient where bounty has been rare, cooks have learned to satisfy with artistry and to beautify scarcity.

COOK THE SIMPLE, TIME-TESTED WAY

Modern kitchen equipment and food-preserving processes have been adopted wherever practical in the Orient. But in most homes, even in large cities, food preparation still goes on much as it did hundreds of years ago.

This is partly because highly sophisticated cuisines were developed using primitive equipment and methods of preservation. Poverty was responsible. A shortage of fuel and food shaped what was used and how. Imagination was the only ingredient in ample supply. Oriental cookery is a triumph of mind over matter.

The shortage of fuel shaped where food was cooked and how. Wood or charcoal were always in short supply in these countries with large populations. The fire that was used for heating the house was also used for cooking. Methods of cooking were developed which took little time or low heat, and therefore less fuel. There was never enough fuel to fire a home oven, indoors or out. So almost all Oriental home cooking is done over a single, all-purpose source of heat. Even today, breads and pastries are prepared at home by steaming, pan-frying, deep-frying, or assembling pre-cooked ingredients. Anything baked or roasted usually is prepared by commercial enterprises.

Because of this centuries-long use of a certain kind of heat source, modern ranges are not completely satisfactory for some types of Oriental cooking. Some electric surface units do not produce controllable heat intense enough for the best Chinese stir-fry cooking, although they can be used adequately. Gas, which can be turned up or down at will, is better if there is enough of it. Special restaurant equipment with bigger gas lines is installed in many restaurants in this country.

Modern oven broilers do not brown, flavor, and glaze the way charcoal or wood fires do. But fortunately, barbecues and braziers are so popular that most Americans have them to use.

Just as the stove for cooking has always been simple, so have the cooking utensils. Most people could not afford many. Only a few kinds of spatulas, ladles, mortars, graters, and pans are essential. Most of the magic is worked with nothing but knives and a chopping block. Basic equipment is so simple that you probably will not need to buy a single item.

Modern electric rice cookers and deep-fat thermometers are useful, but not necessary. There are simple ways to time the rice to perfection or to test the heat of oil. If you use modern cooking equipment, it is by choice, not necessity.

Methods of preserving food have not changed either. They have just been supplemented. Now you can buy certain things canned, frozen, or in mix form. Packaging may be modern, but often the contents have been prepared by the most ancient methods—drying, fermenting, pickling, salting, or sugaring.

It is these strange and aromatic preserved foods that give Oriental cookery its distinctive flavors and infinite variety. Unfortunately, these also confound and often repel American cooks. Some of these foods are not even considered edible, whether they be dried lily flowers, seaweed, or worst of all, the nest of a bird.

But, just as fuel has been scarce for centuries, so has food. Everything nutritious has been preserved for winter or lean times. All these strange ingredients, and the skillful way they are used, speak of a long struggle to survive.

When you cook Oriental food, even in the most glistening modern kitchen, you usually proceed in an ancient way. The Oriental people are noted for their respect of tradition, ancestors, and history. Although they are quick to grasp whatever is useful in the present, they do not turn their backs on the past, even in the kitchen.

AN INGREDIENT SHOPPING GUIDE

How special foods look...are labelled...are sold

For cooking most of the recipes in this book, you do not need any unusual ingredients, or good substitutes are recommended.

Nevertheless, hundreds of strange and puzzling foods are sold at Oriental stores. Cooking with them is not difficult, but just getting to know them is a problem.

This section will try to give you all the help possible to know what foods look like, where you can buy them, how they are packaged, and how to use them.

Fortunately, more and more labels on packages and canned foods now provide both an English and Oriental name for the food, and sometimes a picture and cooking instructions. The U.S. government requires that labels on prepared foods list in English all ingredients in the order of quantity contained.

Certain foods may be eaten only in China or Japan or Korea. But often, the same or similar foods are used by all countries. For this reason, ingredients are described by type (such as sauces or vegetables) so that comparisons can be made which will be useful when you shop. Also, many stores specializing in the foods of a particular country carry products of the others. Korean products are available at Chinese or Japanese stores.

The common English name for each ingredient is given in bold type, followed by words *approximating* the pronunciations of its Oriental names in cases where it would be useful to know them. The Cantonese dialect has been used for Chinese. To avoid confusion, **(C) identifies Chinese names and (J) the Japanese.**

At the end of paragraphs describing unusual ingredients, page numbers are given for recipes including them. Not all foodstuffs discussed are called for in recipes here, but the information given will help you have a better understanding of Far Eastern cookery.

Pictures on pages 10, 13, and 15 show you what some of the important foods look like.

STAPLE INGREDIENTS FOR ALL THE ORIENT

Rice. This is such a staff of life that leaving a single uneaten grain in the rice bowl is regarded as bad manners.

Several kinds exist, which are classified as **short-grain, medium-grain, or long-grain rice.**

Long-grain—sometimes labelled Patna, Bluebonnet, or Rexora—is the type generally sold in America, but the other two types are available at most ordinary groceries now. Calrose, Blue Rose, Japan Rose, Kokuho, Nato, Magnolia, and Zenith are label names you will see for medium-grain rice. California Pearl, Calora, and Colusa are short-grain.

Recipes specify the type required. Long-grain and short-grain are not interchangeable—long-grain needs twice as much water to cook.

A special sticky, glutinous rice, usually only at Oriental stores, is used for certain dumplings, noodles, and pastries. Be sure not to buy it— labelled **"sweet rice," naawr mai (C), or mochi gome (J).** No recipes in this book require it and it cannot be substituted for the other rices.

Noodles. Legend has it that macaroni products were brought to Europe from the Orient. Whatever the facts, noodles have been eaten in the Far East perhaps as long ago as 5,000 B.C. and definitely since 600 B.C.

Most Oriental noodles do not contain egg, but the American government requires that egg be an ingredient before the word "noodles" can appear on a label. Therefore, non-egg noodles are often labelled "imitation noodles" or "alimentary paste" to get around this limited idea of what noodles are.

Noodles in all the countries range from as thin and fine as vermicelli to wide sheets of dough.

Various types of dry noodles are photographed on the next page.

For most of the packaged dry noodles, you will have to visit Oriental stores, but Italian or American products are mentioned as substitutes.

Some Oriental stores stock freshly made versions, refrigerated or frozen. Three-inch **won ton noodle (C)** squares are frequently available fresh, sometimes even at supermarkets that stock many gourmet foods. (Won ton recipe, page 62; used in recipes on pages 34, 40, and 91)

In spite of the variety of national names and packaging, noodles come in just a few main styles. Noodles of wheat or rice flour—with or without egg—may be thin and round like vermicelli and spaghetti, or wide and flat somewhat like the ordinary American egg noodle or Italian fettucine.

The general word for **Chinese noodles** is **mein,** pronounced **meen (C).** Both the thin, round and the wide, flat types may be labelled nothing more than "mein." Sometimes another word precedes mein to indicate the type, but it is safer to look at the noodles or ask the clerk to be sure of the size. Names for **wide, flat noodles** are **chow fun** or **foon tiu meen (C).** *Fun* in the name indicates the noodles are traditionally made of rice (although other starches may be substituted). (Mein, pages 41, 46, 58, 61, 62)

Japanese versions are **thin, round noodles, somen (J),** and **wide, flat noodles, udon (J).** Although these may look just like Chinese mein, they usually cook quicker. (Somen, page 77)

Occasionally flavorers are added to noodles. Resembling spaghetti, **shrimp noodles, haar chee meen (C),** are colored brown and flavored with shrimp. A Japanese type which resembles them, **buckwheat noodles, soba (J),** gets color and flavor from buckwheat flour, also used in the **Korean neng myun.** Italian spinach noodles are a fair substitute for these. (Shrimp noodles, page 61)

Several types of very **thin somen** are colored yellow with egg yolk or green with powdered green tea. Sold in bundles bound with brocade tape, these are the world's most beautiful noodles.

To cook any of these noodles: If the package does not give cooking time, begin testing for doneness just a minute or two after you put the noodles in boiling, salted water. Some cook very quickly and others may take 10 minutes.

To sample noodles a typical way: Drain and serve in hot chicken broth with a dash of soy sauce. Top with such foods as cooked shrimp or chicken, canned abalone slices, canned bamboo shoot slices, mushrooms, briefly-cooked edible-pod or shelled peas, or sliced green onion tops.

Another type of noodle popularly called **"instant" noodles** comes in blocks, curiously twisted or coiled. These are pre-cooked so that they are ready to eat after just a minute or two of boiling, or even just a soaking in boiling water. Sometimes these come with dry soup stock base mixed in or pellets like bouillon cubes so that you can prepare hot noodle soup almost instantly. The Chinese may label these **yee fu meen,** or "tourist" or "picnic" noodles because they are handy for preparing anywhere. The Japanese labels are of infinite variety and are described on page 83.

The only types really strange to Americans are the **translucent noodles,** most of which look like stiff nylon fishing line. (Variations may be wide and coiled, in blocks, or foot-wide discs.) These may be made from dried mung beans, rice, potatoes, or a taro-like root vegetable. Whatever the starch ingredient, these become slippery and soft when soaked in water about 30 minutes. Then they usually are cooked with other ingredients in dishes like Sukiyaki.

Almost all the dry and uncooked translucent noodles may be broken apart and dropped a few at a time into hot oil, whereupon they explode into crisp, white strands that make a beautiful garnish. (The Japanese shirataki made from the taro-like vegetable will *not* explode this way.)

Translucent noodle labels and names may be **bai fun, ning fun, mai fun, or fun see (C),** and **shirataki, harusame (J),** or names similar to the Chinese. They also are referred to as **bean threads, yam noodles, rice sticks, long rice, silver threads, and cellophane or transparent noodles.** (Translucent noodles, pages 57 and 80)

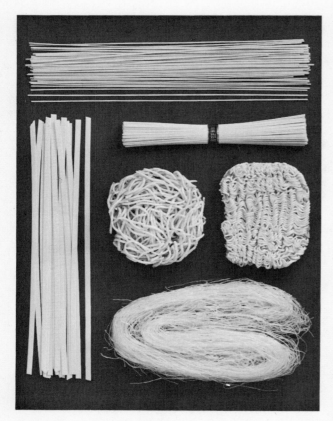

TYPES OF NOODLES (described on the preceding page) are thin and round (two varieties at the top of the photograph), wide and flat (at left), "instant" (two blocks in center), and translucent (loop at bottom).

Flours and Thickeners. Wheat flour is the ingredient of most noodles and is used for dumplings, pastries, and even some breads. Wheat has always been a major staple in northern parts of the Far East, and modern shipping has increased its importance everywhere. Rice flour also is much used.

Cornstarch is used in America for thickening sauces because it cooks clear, unlike wheat flour which remains murky. It also gives a crisper texture to coatings on fried foods. Water chestnut flour, used in the Orient and occasionally available here, acts much like cornstarch.

The gelatin used is **agar-agar, dai choy goh (C), or kanten (J),** made from seaweed. Unlike the gelatin in America made from animals, this does not melt at room temperature. It is sold in several forms at Oriental stores, usually crinkly, translucent, oblong blocks.

Oils and Fats. Vegetable oil is an essential. Any of the salad oils works well, except perhaps olive oil, which has a distinctive taste. A little **sesame oil** is added sometimes to dishes or mixed with other oils for its nutty, concentrated flavor. Oriental and health food stores sell it (some at health food stores is refined to have no odor or flavor). (Sesame oil, pages 42, 47, 48, 50, 61, 63, 78, 80, 81)

Shortening and butter are not used for most dishes, but lard is often used.

Sweeteners. Although intensely sweet dishes and desserts are not numerous, a little sugar, honey, or sweet rice wine may be added to many dishes to bring out flavor or to glaze. Sherry is a good substitute for the wine in all the cuisines; but Japanese amber **sweet rice wine, mirin (J),** sometimes labelled "sweet sake," and the **white rice wine, sake (J),** are widely available at Oriental, gourmet, and large liquor stores. Chinese wines are available in this country at a few Chinese stores. (Mirin, pages 74, 75, 78, 80, 82; sake, pages 33, 75, 76, 79, 81, 82, 84, 88)

Vinegars. American white vinegar is the most all-purpose, but cider vinegar can sometimes be used. For most authentic taste, use imported products from Oriental stores.

A particularly delicious Chinese type labelled **"red vinegar," jit choh (C),** is customarily a dipping sauce for crisp egg rolls or other oily foods. You needn't purchase Chinese **white vinegar, baak choh (C),** because it is much like American white vinegar.

Japanese **white rice vinegar, su (J),** is sweeter and milder than American vinegar. (White rice vinegar, pages 54, 71, 84)

A FEW IMPORTANT SPICES & HERBS

Garlic and onions are very important seasoners in many dishes.

The black pepper used in America is not the kind generally used in the Far East and may give an undesirable non-Oriental appearance to some foods. However, white pepper is used in Canton. **Red peppers** (chiles) in varying degrees of hotness are frequently employed in northern China and Korea and are an ingredient in the **Japanese seasoning, togarashi,** which also contains sesame seed, orange peel, and a Japanese pepper. (Togarashi, page 80)

The **Oriental pepper, fah chiu (C) or sansho (J),** comes from berries or leaves of Zanthoxylum plants. Another plant, Perilla, produces the **jee soh (C) or shiso (J) pepper leaf,** used fresh or dried and powdered.

Ginger root, geung (C) or **shoga (J),** adds zip to all the cuisines.

A large amount of **fresh ginger root,** raw or cooked, is very hot and nippy. But a little merely enhances flavor, just as a little garlic does. The fresh light-brown, iris-like root is at many supermarkets regularly. See photograph on page 13.

To keep fresh ginger root for several weeks, just refrigerate unwrapped. Or freeze for longer storage (you can grate or cut off what you need without thawing).

Don't substitute dried ground ginger unless the recipe says to. However, you can make an acceptable substitute for fresh root. (Fresh ginger is used in a multitude of recipes in this book.) Buy dry *whole* ginger, packaged by several spice companies. Put pieces of dry ginger in a jar and cover with water. Soak several days, or until the pieces have swollen and are completely moist within.

Ginger also is **preserved** in syrup (sold in bottles) and **candied** or crystallized in sugar (in cellophane packages or bottles). You can buy these at regular groceries. (Preserved ginger, page 65; candied, 50, 65)

Pickled ginger, soon geung (C) or **beni shoga (J),** may be found at Oriental or gourmet shops in bottles or cans. It may be white or tinted red or pink. (Pickled red ginger, page 84)

Chinese parsley, yuen sai, is not curly like regular parsley and tastes much different. The Japanese seldom use it, but do use regular parsley for garnish. See photograph on page 13.

Chinese parsley really is the coriander spice plant, which you can grow by planting whole coriander seed. At Mexican-American markets it goes by the name of *cilantro* and at Japanese markets by "Chinese parsley." Sometimes you can find it at supermarkets. (Chinese parsley, pages 35, 38, 40, 44, 46, 48, 50, 52, 59, 82)

Sesame seed, chih mah (C) or **goma (J),** may be our ordinary white kind or coal-black. **Black sesame** of the same size and shape usually is only at Oriental markets, called **hak chih mah (C)** or **kuro goma (J).** Its flavor is more pungent.

Curry powder is a spice mixture which has caught on in both China and Japan for non-Indian dishes. Use whatever blend you have. (Curry powder, pages 42, 53)

Chinese "five-spice," ng heung fun, is a blend of ground cloves, fennel, licorice root, cinnamon, and **star anise, baht ghok (C).** An American spice company bottles five-spice, but visit a Chinese store for the anise in its beautiful, star-shaped whole form. (Five-spice, pages 33, 42, 54)

BROTHS & SAUCES, SIMPLE OR EXOTIC

The liquid in many sauces may be just water or meat broth. Chicken broth is especially favored. Preparations similar to American chicken stock base also are sold in the Far East. Canned broth is handy.

In most of Japan, except inland or mountain areas, a broth called **Dashi (J),** made by boiling **dried bonito fish, katsuobushi,** and **dried tangle seaweed, kombu,** is essential to various dishes. You can buy bags containing the prepared ingredients, labelled **Dashi-no-moto,** for brewing Dashi as easily as you make tea. (Dashi, pages 71, 73, 74, 76, 81, 82)

Soy sauce, see yow (C) or **shoyu (J),** is made by a complicated process of fermenting soy beans—and toasted wheat or wheat flour. Chinese soy sauce is the saltiest and made mostly just from beans. The Japanese sauce is less salty and sweeter due to the large amount of toasted wheat employed. Japanese-style sauce is the most widely marketed (at almost all stores) and the most all-purpose—it has been used for testing nearly all the recipes in this book.

Several **Chinese soy sauces** are imported: **sang chow (C),** which is lighter in color than the Japanese sauce, **tow chow (C),** which is darker with a slight molasses tang, and **jee yow (C),** which is thick like molasses and bitterish (don't buy this kind).

Other sauces have beans as a base. In Japan **fermented soy bean paste, miso (J),** is a thickener for many soups, a barbecue sauce, and even a salad dressing. It comes in two forms—mild white or pungent brick-red—in cartons, tubs, or cans at Oriental shops. It keeps indefinitely unrefrigerated. (White miso bean paste, page 74)

Chinese stores sell a variety of sauces based on beans. Salty "yellow" or brown **bean sauce, meen see jeong (C),** is canned or bottled. Reddish, slightly sweet bean **hoi sin sauce, hoi sin jeong (C),** also canned, is seasoned with garlic and chiles. (Bean sauce, pages 44, 48; hoi sin sauce, pages 59, 60)

Salty **fermented black beans, dow see (C),** to use for sauces come whole, usually in plastic bags. (Fermented black beans, pages 47, 50, 53, 56)

Several bottled sauces have seafood as a base: **Chinese shrimp sauce, hom harh; fish sauce, yu low;** and **oyster sauce, hoh yow,** which you can sometimes find at gourmet shops. (Oyster sauce, pages 43, 58, 59, 60, 61)

(Continued on next page)

Canned Chinese **plum sauce, soh mui jeong (C)**, often is a spicy accompaniment to roast duck and sometimes labelled "duck sauce." (Plum sauce, pages 52, 59, 60)

All the countries enjoy a simple **hot mustard sauce** made by blending our ordinary ground dry (yellow) mustard with water to paste consistency. This mustard also can be substituted in recipes calling for the Japanese **green "horseradish," wasabi (J)** (actually the root of a type of cabbage), sold powdered in small cans at Japanese stores to be mixed with water. (Wasabi, pages 69, 84)

INGREDIENTS TO SEASON & FLAVOR

Some "minor" ingredients are used more for flavor than as a main ingredient for food value.

Seaweed often may just be a flavorer, although it is highly nutritive in small amounts. Most people think of seaweed as typical of Japanese cuisine, but China has also made use of this easily dried product. A **hair-like seaweed, faht choy (C)**, is one of the numerous foods in the Buddhist vegetarian dish, Jai. Paper-thin rectangles of dried purple-black **laver seaweed, gee choy (C)**, flavor soup.

This same dried **laver seaweed, nori (J)** is a wrapping for Japanese rice rolls and a garnish for numerous foods. In Korea, called *kim*, it is toasted and served at most meals.

Tough, gray, dried **tangle seaweed, kombu (J)**, is essential to the Japanese broth, Dashi. Other seaweeds are tied in decorative shapes and simmered in stews and still others are dried and ground to sprinkle on food. At Japanese stores, you can buy small bottles of ground seaweed, some mixed with other seasoners.

Citrus fruits are not as widely used for flavoring as they are in cookery of other countries. Oranges and tangerines or Mandarin oranges generally are eaten whole and fresh. Seafood seldom is accompanied with lemon. But the Japanese use citrus peel to garnish and flavor soups. And the Chinese have found that **dried tangerine peel, gwoh pay (C)**, imparts a sweet-tart flavor to a variety of things. You can buy the peel by the ounce at Chinese stores. (Dried tangerine peel, pages 39, 40, 50, 57)

The Chinese stores also sell an infinite assortment of other dried foods to flavor. Two of these are called for in recipes here: patent-leathery, maroon **"red dates," hong joh (C)**; and **dried duck gizzard, ahp sun (C)**. (Red dates, pages 50, 57; duck gizzard, page 40)

ANIMAL PRODUCTS FROM LAND OR SEA

Meat, Fowl, and Eggs. Practically every kind of poultry and meat, including lamb, is used from tail to toe. Pork and chicken are most popular.

At Chinese meat shops you can buy spicy **pork sausages, lop cheong (C)**, about 5 inches long. They must be simmered or steamed 15 minutes, or until the fat is translucent. You can cook them right in with plain rice. (Chinese sausage, pages 37, 47)

A whole **roast pig, siu yok (C)**, often is hung from a hook; buy it on the bone by the pound. To sample, heat pieces in a very hot oven and serve with Chinese oyster sauce for a dip. Glazed **barbecued pork, chahr siu (C)**, also purchased by the pound, can merely be sliced and served cold with hot mustard sauce. (Barbecued pork, recipe on page 33; used on pages 37, 83)

You can also buy whole (or parts of) **roast ducks** and **chickens**, and whole **squab**.

Preserved duck eggs from Chinese groceries are curiosities that, to be frank, you may not like. **Hundred (or thousand)-year-old eggs, pay dahn (C)**, have been preserved for just 100 days, during which they turn brown. Wash off the black coating and shell. Slice or cut in wedges; serve with pickled onions and pickled red ginger, or a "red" vinegar dip, for appetizers. **Salted duck eggs, hahm dahn (C)**, have been brine-cured about 40 days. Boil them 20 to 30 minutes before shelling. Eat hot with rice, or cut in wedges as a cold relish.

Fish, Shellfish, and Sea Animals. Every kind of edible fish or shellfish from sea or fresh water is relished. Such things as eel, jellyfish, squid, octopus, and cuttlefish are used fresh, canned, dried, salted, or preserved however possible.

Dried fish and shrimp are used everywhere for broths and soup stock. The Japanese toast tiny dried fish for a crispy treat.

One unusual form of fish Americans like readily is the Japanese **steamed fish cake, kamaboko (J)**. White fish is pressed into a half-cylinder, often tinted red on top. Buy it at Oriental markets in cans or fresh from refrigerated displays. To sample, just slice and serve cold as a side dish. (Steamed fish cake, pages 73, 83, 90)

Canned **clams** and **oysters** from the Orient can be different and delicious varieties. Some, either smoked or in soy sauce and ready to eat, are at gourmet shops or supermarkets.

The canned **abalone** sold at most groceries here is useful for an appetizer (just slice and skewer) and in cooked dishes.

UNUSUAL VEGETABLES SOLD AT ORIENTAL MARKETS

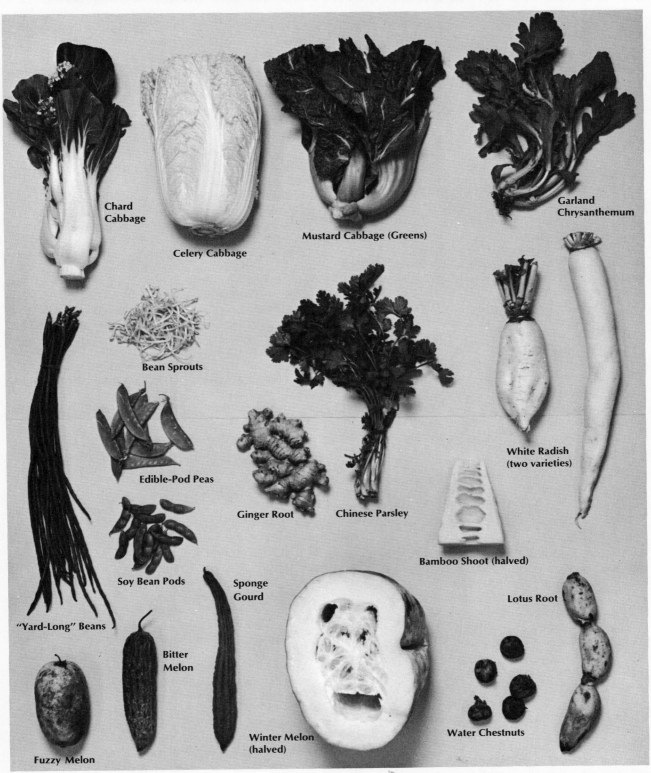

Chard Cabbage

Celery Cabbage

Mustard Cabbage (Greens)

Garland Chrysanthemum

Bean Sprouts

Edible-Pod Peas

Ginger Root

Chinese Parsley

White Radish (two varieties)

Bamboo Shoot (halved)

Soy Bean Pods

Sponge Gourd

Lotus Root

"Yard-Long" Beans

Bitter Melon

Winter Melon (halved)

Water Chestnuts

Fuzzy Melon

INTRIGUING VEGETABLES are described, with shopping information, on pages 14 through 16.

VEGETABLES, PICKLES, BEAN CAKES & MUSHROOMS

Nearly all of the fresh vegetables discussed here are photographed on page 13.

Not all of these are necessary for recipes in this book, but you will be curious about what they are when you see them in Oriental markets.

Although some other types of unusual Oriental foods take time to get to like, the vegetables are pleasing to nearly everyone at first taste.

Beans, Peas, and Bean Cakes. The same fresh green beans and shelled peas common in the United States are eaten, plus other varieties.

In fact, legumes probably rival rice as a staple food. In addition, they provide protein as well as starch.

Very thin **"yard-long" beans, dow ghok (C)** or **sasage (J),** occasionally appear at supermarkets. (Yard-long beans, 43)

Edible-pod peas, hoh laan dow (C) or **saya endo (J),** also are known as sugar, snow or Chinese pea pods. These are sold fresh and in packages frozen at some supermarkets. Fresh ones should be "strung" the way you do green beans. (Edible-pod peas, pages 48, 55, 59, 78, 79, 82, 83)

If you can't find edible-pod peas, you can prepare a substitute from ordinary fresh green peas (the kind you shell). Their pods are edible *if* you strip off a thin, tough membrane inside. To do this:

Shell peas. Hold each half of the pod about 1 inch from its stem end. Fold the pod in toward the lining. This will break the crisp, edible outside portion, but not the tough inside membrane.

Holding onto the stem end with one hand and the pod with the other, gently pull the membrane down and away from the pod. It usually will come off in one sheet.

With practice, you will acquire the knack of preparing the pods very quickly. If they break or do not strip easily, throw them away.

These pea pods take slightly longer to cook than the whole edible-pod kind.

In Japanese markets you may see frozen green **soy bean pods, eda mame (J).** These are already cooked. Just boil several minutes to thaw and heat, then salt, shell, and eat as snack or appetizer.

Dried beans of infinite variety and color exist. Tiny olive-green **mung beans, lok dow (C)** or **moyashi mame (J),** 1/8-inch-long, are sprouted for the familiar **bean sprouts, ngaah choy (C)** or **moyashi (J).** You can buy these at Oriental markets and sprout your own—see box on this page.

Fresh sprouts are now in the vegetable sections of many supermarkets, loose or bagged. Canned ones are everywhere. At Oriental stores, you may also see a bigger, crunchier sprout with large bean attached, a soy bean. This is used differently; don't substitute for bean sprouts. (Bean sprouts, pages 55, 60, 91)

Dried beans, usually red ones, already mashed and sweetened for pastry fillings, are sold canned by Chinese and Japanese stores labelled **sweet bean paste or prepared red bean flour, koshian (J).** Black and yellow forms also are prepared. (Sweetened bean paste, page 66)

Sweetened boiled or salted parched beans and peas for appetizers or side dishes may be purchased in cans or plastic packages at Japanese markets.

Bean cakes are a major food item. They are compressed from the milky liquid pressed out of cooked soy beans. (See photograph on page 15.)

Fresh bean cake, dow foo (C) or **tofu (J),** is white with the texture of well-baked custard. At Oriental stores and occasional supermarkets, you will find it cut in blocks—often refrigerated and in water. Dow foo is firmer than tofu, but another version is softer: **"water" bean cake, suey dow foo (C).** Some Chinese stores sell tofu for suey dow foo, but there is a difference. Tofu is firmer.

All countries also utilize **fried bean cake.** The Chinese type comes in small cubes, **dow foo pok (C).** The Japanese fried type, **aburaage (J),** may be a brown hollow square or sausage shape. See photo opposite.

HOW TO GROW BEAN SPROUTS

Using a baking pan with 1½ to 2-inch sides, cover the bottom with four smooth layers of clean burlap cut to size. Sprinkle about a half cup of tiny, dried, olive-green *mung beans* over the sacking. Mung beans are described on this page.

Saturate the whole thing with water and pour off any excess. Water daily or when the top layer dries out.

To sprout beans successfully, keep them at a relatively constant temperature (68° to 70°) in a dark place free from dirt or oil that may be in the air from cooking.

The beans sprout within two or three days and are ready in five to seven days, when they are a little more than an inch long.

Rinse the sprouts in a bowl of water or colander to remove husks, and dry well. Refrigerate up to three days in a plastic bag.

Other forms of bean cake are fermented in wine, broiled, baked, and dried. Don't substitute the Chinese bean cake in bottles for fresh bean cake (this is fermented and in alcohol, has a strong flavor).

(Fresh bean cake, dow foo or tofu, pages 48, 59, 73, 79, 80, 91; suey dow foo, page 39; dow foo pok, page 47)

Vegetables and Pickles. A great many of our vegetables are used. But you will see different varieties in Oriental markets (sometimes even supermarkets) of such things as eggplant, broccoli, spinach, cabbage, radishes, cucumbers, and squash.

Oriental **eggplant** are long and thin, with few seeds. They range from as small as pickling cucumbers to a foot long. Sometimes supermarkets carry them.

The **spinach** at Oriental markets may have a different leaf and stem structure; if it tastes like spinach, use it the same way. Resembling spinach but with notched leaves, Japanese **garland chrysanthemum, shungiku (J),** has flavor mildly like the flower smells. (Garland chrysanthemum, pages 80, 82)

Three kinds of greens are found, which will be referred to as celery cabbage, chard cabbage, and mustard cabbage. See photo on page 13.

Celery cabbage, wong nga bok or siu choy (C) or hakusai (J), is also called Chinese or nappa cabbage. It has a delicate celery-cabbage taste. It consists of a solid, oblong head of wide, celery-like stalks ending in frilly, pale-green leaves. Many supermarkets sell it. (Celery cabbage, pages 42, 57, 59, 79, 80)

Chard cabbage, baak choy (C) or shirona (J), looks much like Swiss chard. It consists of a clump of snow-white stalks ending in wide, dark-green leaves. You may find it at supermarkets in areas with Oriental population. Some people also call it Chinese cabbage. (Chard cabbage, page 42)

Mustard cabbage, gai choy (C) or karashina (J), has a mustard flavor milder than that of ordinary mustard greens. It consists of a clump of fat, apple-green stalks ending in darker apple-green leaves. Usually you must go to Oriental markets for it, where it may also be called mustard greens or root. (Mustard cabbage, pages 38, 42)

Pickled versions of these cabbages are popular in all the countries and may be bought at Oriental markets in cans or bottles, from barrels, or in refrigerated plastic bags.

A giant **white radish, loh baak (C) or daikon (J),** is very crisp, tender, mild, and sweet—much like a turnip in flavor. The variety preferred by Japanese may be more than a foot long. The Chinese type is shorter, squat, and slightly more fibrous.

BEAN CAKES, described on these pages, are dow foo (top left); dow foo pok (top right); aburaage (center and lower right); and tofu (lower left).

But the two varieties may be used interchangeably. Sometimes supermarkets carry them. They keep many days if refrigerated in plastic bags. (White radishes, pages 69, 82)

One of the most popular Japanese pickles, called **takuan,** is made from white radish. You can buy the pickle—often tinted yellow—in cans, bottles, or refrigerated plastic bags.

Several unusual types of squash, melons, and gourds are available at Oriental shops.

The **Japanese squash, kabocha,** is pumpkin-like inside but with green, ridged skin.

The balsam pear or **Chinese bitter melon, foo gwah (C) or nigauri (J),** is the size of a cucumber and brilliant green. It has a bitter flavor, but is relished stuffed or stir-fried with meat.

The **Chinese fuzzy or hairy melon, moh gwah or jchee gwah (C),** is sweet-flavored, a 6-inch oval shape, with gray-green, fuzzy skin. (Fuzzy melon, page 39)

Winter melon, doong gwah (C) or togan (J), resembles a watermelon, but its flesh is white and firmer. (Winter melon, page 40)

The **sponge gourd, see gwah (C) or hechima (J),** is sometimes called Chinese okra or luffa. It is about a foot long, green, with deep lengthwise grooves. The Japanese make much use of a **dried gourd, kampyo (J),** which looks like strips of rawhide in its cellophane-packaged form.

Chinese **sweet pickles, tzahp choy (C),** sold in cans, consist of mixed vegetables such as cucumber, melon, carrot, and ginger. Cut in slivers, they make a pretty garnish for any sweet-and-sour dish.

Many unusual root vegetables are at Oriental markets, too. Japanese **burdock, gobo (J),** is several feet long and very thin, with brown skin. Taros of various sizes resemble potatoes and are used by Chinese and Japanese.

Bamboo shoots, suehn (C) or takenoko (J), are familiar to you as they come canned. But you may find fresh whole or cut shoots in a tub of water at Oriental markets. Like canned shoots, these should be cooked very briefly.

Although you can buy canned ones everywhere, you may enjoy the sweeter flavor and crisper texture of fresh **water chestnuts, mah tai (C) or kuwai (J).** These are dark brown, scaly, and look something like a narcissus bulb. To prepare, just pare off the thin skin and use as if canned. See photograph on page 13.

One of the most beautiful exotic vegetables at Oriental markets is **lotus root, lien ngow (C) or renkon or hasu (J).** It looks like a string of fat, brown, link sausages. Peeled and sliced crosswise, it is white with symmetrical holes that make it look like a snowflake. If simmered, it is bland much like a potato. You also can slice it very thin and deep fry like potato chips for an appetizer. (Lotus root, page 82)

Lotus seeds, lien jee (C), in cellophane packages at Chinese stores, are shaped like large dried white corn kernels. (Lotus seeds, page 40)

Mushrooms. The mushrooms sold fresh or canned in America appear in many dishes, as do the **dried mushrooms** you can buy at most groceries now (Italian ones can be substituted). Several types and sizes are dried but the most common names for **dried mushrooms** are **doong gwoo (C) or shiitake (J).** (Dried mushrooms, pages 35, 38, 39, 40, 47, 48, 50, 51, 56, 57, 79, 84, 92)

The intriguing **straw mushroom, chao gwoo (C),** may be bought canned or dried in Chinese stores. It consists of a "bud" containing a miniature mushroom. The Japanese love the tiny **"slippery" mushroom, nameko (J),** canned in its own jelly-like liquid and used for soup. (Straw mushrooms, page 80)

A crinkly **dried black fungus, wohn yee (C) or kikurage (J),** can be bought at Chinese stores. It has a crisper texture than a dried mushroom after soaking in water and swells to an "ear" shape responsible for the Chinese name meaning "cloud ear."

SOME INTRIGUING FRUITS & NUTS

Because the Oriental countries cover a vast area and range of climates, numerous fruits and nuts are grown.

Different fruit varieties such as **white "snow" peaches** and crisp **pears** from Japan are available, canned in syrup. Such exotics as **kumquats, mangoes,** and **loquats** also are canned in syrup. A recipe for preserving kumquats is on page 66.

Litchi "nuts" (pronounced **lie chee),** and the smaller **longans** (called **lohng ngahn (C),** meaning "dragon's eye") may be found dried in the shell or fresh-canned in syrup. Litchi may also be spelled "lychee" or "lichee."

The shells of the dried ones are thin, round, brown, and bumpy. Dried litchi fruit looks and tastes something like a prune, but dried longans have a medicinal flavor. Both canned litchis and longans resemble canned white cherries or grapes. (Litchis and longans, pages 50, 65)

Gingko nuts, baak gwoah (C) or ginnan (J), sold here shelled in cans, are oval and resemble garbanzo beans in color and flavor.

All these canned fruits and nuts may be found at gourmet as well as Oriental shops. Some Chinese restaurants sell packages of dried litchis.

In Japanese stores, you will see tiny red or green pickled **plums, ume (J).** Japanese eat one or two for breakfast with rice and miso soup. Chinese versions seldom sold here are various colors and eaten the same way.

TOOLS & UTENSILS, HOW TO USE THEM

Cooking and serving with equipment you own or may buy

If every tool, utensil, and dish from the Far East were illustrated, this book would look like a mail-order catalog.

However, about 50 of the most important or useful items have been sketched on pages 20 and 21 of this chapter.

On the following pages are descriptions of these items with information about how to use them. **Names of items sketched are in bold type.**

This will help you shop with confidence, even in stores where the clerks may not know much about cooking—or the English language.

However, you don't *need* any of these items to cook and serve.

YOU ALREADY OWN THE ESSENTIAL EQUIPMENT

Undoubtedly you have in your kitchen right now all the tools and cooking utensils necessary for almost every recipe in this book. You probably own plenty of dishes which are suitable for serving.

All you need to cook is an assortment of sauce-pans in varying sizes and a large, deep frying pan. You can even improvise a steamer from pans you have.

Kitchen tools required are likewise few and simple. You can do very well with no more than a slotted spoon, a pancake turner, a grater and shredder, thin skewers, a wire strainer, and a large knife with a wedge-shaped blade.

Because dishes used for serving in the various Oriental countries vary so—from ornate porcelain to rustic pottery—you probably already own dishes which will set the proper mood. To enhance them, you can add bamboo mats, a table runner of brocade, or patterned cloths to create a feeling of a particular country. Then decorate with flowers of the Orient such as chrysanthemums or fruit-tree blossoms, fresh fruit, or leaves.

You do not need to buy anything new to prepare and serve Oriental food. What you do need is will power to resist buying all the beautiful and fascinating things available.

USEFUL BUT OPTIONAL TOOLS & KITCHEN AIDS

The Wok, for Stir-Frying, Steaming, and Deep-Frying. If you buy only one cooking utensil, it probably should be the spherical-bottomed **Chinese wok,** mainly used for dishes cooked by what is called the stir-fry method.

A wok has other uses. You can put a round cake rack inside to improvise a steamer or just place the stack bamboo steamers (sketched on page 20) over water. A wok is excellent for deep-frying—you need less oil because the pan has a spherical bottom.

This is how you use the wok for stir-frying: Stir-fry dishes, called *chow* in Chinese and sometimes "toss-cooked" or "sautéed" in English, may consist of meat, chicken, or seafood cut in small pieces and vegetables cut in similar-sized pieces (so everything will cook quickly). A sauce is cooked with the dish which consists of oil; seasoners such as garlic and ginger; liquid such as water, broth, wine or soy sauce (or combinations); and sometimes cornstarch for thickening.

Prepare all the ingredients as the recipe says and line them up in the order you will add them to the pan. The cooking takes several minutes only and you cannot stop to prepare anything or you will ruin the dish. Cook each thing just as the recipe says, being careful not to overcook.

Stir-frying is designed to cook protein foods thoroughly, but leave them tender and juicy; stir-

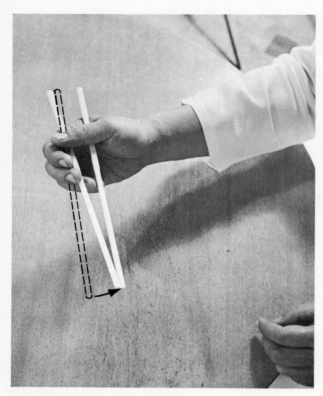

CHOPSTICKS *are held this way, so that the inside stick is stationary and the outside one moves, forming pincers for picking up small pieces of food.*

The wok in the sketch on page 20 has loop handles, one on each side. Another type is made with just one long wooden handle. A loop-handled wok has better balance (important if you also use it for deep-frying), but the one-handled kind is practical because you can pour out the contents quickly to prevent overcooking.

Buy a large wok, at least 14 or 15 inches in diameter, so that you can stir and toss vigorously. They are sold at either Chinese or Japanese stores. The lid and ring base are sold separately. (The Japanese name is *shina nabe*, literally "Chinese pan.")

A small wok can be used only for small quantities and doesn't adapt well to other uses. You might as well use a 12-inch frying pan or a Spanish paella pan.

Most woks are not stainless steel and rust easily. Prepare a non-stainless one by scrubbing the inside with steel wool, washing well, and drying thoroughly. Then heat the pan, rub with salad oil inside, and turn off the heat.

A Pan for Deep-Frying; Frying Techniques. Designed for deep-frying, the **Japanese Tempura nabe** has a removable curved rack which fits on one side of the pan for draining the fried foods and keeping them hot (see sketch on page 20).

The size of Tempura nabe generally sold has the same capacity as a 10-inch frying pan but has higher sides. It can substitute for a small wok. Larger sizes sometimes can be found that would be more suitable for using as a wok.

Whether you deep-fry in a Tempura nabe or regular pan, you can test the heat of the oil this way: Drop in a bit of batter or small piece of the food to be fried. If it sinks, the oil is too cool. If it immediately *pops* to the top of the oil and bounces about, beginning to brown, the temperature is right. If it browns almost at once, the oil is too hot.

If you have a thermometer, keep the oil between 350° and 375°. Never let it fall below 350° or the food will be soggy. Remember that food put in the oil cools it.

Rice Cookers, Electric and Otherwise. An electric cooker is useful only if you cook rice often or if you are one of those people who just can't make rice turn out right.

A special rimmed **Japanese saucepan for cooking rice** is used on a regular range (see sketch). The lid which fits tightly down inside a rim creates a tight seal. The rim catches water which boils out. (Japanese begin cooking rice covered over high heat. When water and steam hiss from under the lid, the heat is turned very low.)

frying assures that vegetables will just be cooked until barely tender, yet will retain all their beautiful color and crisp texture.

Very high heat is necessary for the best wok cooking. You may prefer to omit using the ring base sketched on page 20 if you cook on an electric surface unit or if the gas pressure is not high—so that the bottom of the pan will be as close to the heat as possible.

Gas is better because you can turn the heat up or down instantly. If you have an electric range, you may heat two units—one very hot and another medium-hot—so that you can move the pan from one to the other as needed.

Proper stir-frying is a noisy operation with loud hisses, sizzling, and clatter of metal utensils as you stir and toss the food constantly. It is a vigorous operation of fast motion, arm action, and boxer-like footwork. No wonder so many Chinese men become cooks.

Don't worry about getting the wok too hot when you cook—better too hot than not hot enough. It is practically impossible to burn the food if you work fast enough and stir-toss constantly.

Now that you know how a wok is used, you can decide what type and size to buy.

Steamers, To Buy or Improvise. A steamer consists of a pan containing just an inch or so of water with some sort of device for supporting food to be cooked *above* this water. The food may be placed in a dish (if it is soft or has a sauce) or on a perforated tray or rack (if it is firm, such as bread or a whole fish). Then a cover of some sort is placed on the pan.

To steam the food, you heat the water to a simmer, just hot enough to produce steam which circulates inside the covered pan. Steam is hot enough to cook food (it has the same temperature as boiling water).

Although you can buy several types, first consider *improvising a steamer from equipment you have*. You need only four elements: a large pan and cover, a device for supporting the food above the water, and a dish or rack for holding the food.

For the large pan and cover, you can use an electric frying pan with domed lid, regular 11 or 12-inch frying pan with domed lid, a Chinese *wok* described previously which has a high lid, or any large, deep kettle. (If the kettle has no lid, cover it tightly with foil.)

The cover or lid should be 1 or 2 inches above the cooking food so steam can circulate. Put a cloth or dish towel over the top of the kettle before putting the lid on (this prevents condensed water from dripping on the food).

The devices to hold food above the water vary depending on whether you steam the food in a dish, or on a perforated tray or rack.

A dish does not have to be much above the water. So the dish may be supported with canning jar rings, 7-ounce tuna cans with both ends removed, 4 tablespoons with the back sides of the bowls turned up, a trivot, or an inexpensive Chinese steamer stand.

A perforated tray or rack must be supported at least 2 inches above the simmering water so that the water does not bubble up onto the food. Taller cans, such as several 1-pound cans with both ends removed, are excellent supports.

The dish you use for holding foods does not need to be ovenproof, but should have a rim or sides. It must be smaller in diameter than the steamer pan.

The real trick of steam cookery is to remove a hot dish from the steamer without burning your fingers. Hot pads soak up scalding water, and rubber gloves aren't adequately insulated. The best utensil is the three-pronged **steamed dish retriever** sketched on page 20. The next best holder is a simple harness of string that you can make (see photograph on page 46).

The perforated tray or rack may be improvised from a cake-cooling rack, the rack from a pressure cooker, or foil pans with a liberal number of wide slashes in the bottom.

As you can see, there are so many ways to improvise a steamer. But, if you like, you can buy a large metal steaming kettle with rack or an electric steam cooker with rack.

The most attractive steaming aids to buy are the Oriental **bamboo steamer trays** available in several diameters. These stack on top of each other. You can buy each tray separately to get just one or as many as you like, and you also can buy a bamboo lid for the stack separately. (See sketch on page 20.)

If you use the bamboo lid, you do not have to cover the steamer pan (any large kettle, frying pan, or wok). Just support one tray, or a stack of as many as you like, several inches above the simmering water with cans which have both ends removed. If you use these trays in a Chinese wok, you need not support them because the pan is spherical—the trays will rest against the rounded sides several inches above the bottom of the pan and any water in it.

Cook-at-the-Table Equipment, To Buy or Improvise. In the Chinese, Japanese, and Korean sections of this book, you will find recipes for meals cooked at the table in broth simmering in the moat of the charcoal-fired, chimneyed **"hot pot"** (featured on the cover of this book).

Names for the pot are the same as the names of dishes cooked in them. The Chinese names are *Hoh Go, Tan Lo,* or *Dar Bin Lo;* the Japanese, *Shabu Shabu* or *Mitzutaki;* the Korean, *Sin Sul Lo.* The pot is sometimes said to be of Mongolian origin.

Be sure to get one made of metal suitable for cooking, usually brass. Some are designed purely for planters or ornamental use.

This is how you fire a "hot pot": First fill the moat with the hot cooking broth, then half-fill the chimney with glowing charcoal. (Start charcoal briquets outdoors in a heavy bucket which can be carried indoors; transfer coals with tongs.) *Caution:* Be sure to put liquid in the moat before adding coals; otherwise the heat of the charcoal may melt the solder. Close the moat with its cover-top during cooking.

Some cookers are outfitted with chimney covers that may be put on to douse the fire when you're through cooking. If your cooker has no chimney cover, substitute a small dish half-filled with water.

On page 28 you will see photographs of several substitutes for the hot pot—a chafing dish, a heatproof casserole set over an alcohol burner (you also can place a casserole, which should hold two quarts or more, on a charcoal brazier), and an electric saucepan used for deep-frying.

(Continued on page 22)

USEFUL BUT OPTIONAL COOKING EQUIPMENT

Chinese Wok with Lid and Ring Base

Japanese Tempura Nabe

Japanese Saucepan for Rice

Bamboo Steamer Trays (stacked) with Lid on Top

Steamed Dish Retriever

"Hot Pot"

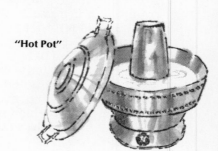

Japanese Sukiyaki Pan

Japanese Hibachi

Genghis Khan Grill

Japanese Suribachi with Wooden Pestle

Japanese Shredder

Fine Grater

Japanese Sudare

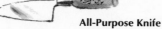

Fish Knife

All-Purpose Knife

Cleaver

Screen-Wire Skimmer

Wire Ladle

Wire Ladle

Ladle

Bamboo Tongs

Chinese Curved Spatula

USEFUL BUT OPTIONAL TOOLS & KITCHEN AIDS

Chinese Chopsticks

Rice-Serving Paddle

Teacups

Japanese Sake Jugs and Cups

Japanese Chopsticks

Chopstick Rests

Ceramic Spoon

Several Styles of Teapots

Korean Metal Rice Bowl

Japanese Rice Bowl

Japanese Soup Bowl

Chinese Rice Bowl

Chinese Soup Bowls

Lidded Rice Buckets

Japanese Chawan Mushi Dish

Japanese Bowls for Salad-Type Foods

Japanese Meshi Donburi

Chinese Platter

Chinese Pedestal Dish

Plates of Various Shapes

Baskets

Stack Lacquer Boxes

Sectioned Lacquer Tray

Metal Stack Boxes

Soy Sauce Pitcher

Teapot-Style Sauce Pitcher

Tiny Condiment Dishes

The saucepan, or an electric frying pan or special electric Japanese *Shabu Shabu* pot, are not glamorous, but the dependable, controlled heat is very handy. And you don't have to go to the trouble of lighting charcoal.

Another popular pan for table cooking is a **Japanese Sukiyaki pan** of heavy iron with an appealing dark burnish. (See sketch on page 20.) Detachable handles can be purchased.

You can use these pans to prepare Sukiyaki at the table over an electric hotplate (an alcohol burner does not produce high-enough heat). An electric Sukiyaki pan or ordinary electric frying pan can be substituted.

A charcoal brazier, commonly known as a **Japanese hibachi,** is useful for warming appetizers, broiling many kinds of foods including those on skewers, and as a heat source for cooking at the table. (This type of brazier is actually called *hichirin* in Japan—an hibachi is another stove used for heating the house.)

A special brazier called a **Genghis Khan grill** (sketched) has a domed grill with narrow slits in it, useful for charcoal-broiling small pieces of food. A rim below the dome catches juices to make a tasty natural dipping sauce.

Unfortunately, few people are aware that burning charcoal indoors can be dangerous if the room is not *very* well ventilated. Charcoal can release carbon monoxide enough to kill or to make people feel groggy or ill.

USEFUL BUT OPTIONAL COOKING EQUIPMENT

If you buy any kitchen tools, first get Oriental knives. For you will spend much more time cutting food than you do cooking it.

A variety are available for a variety of purposes, but two or three types will be sufficient. Three styles are sketched on page 20.

The wedge-shaped-blade style is used for fish in the Orient, but you may consider it good for many purposes—it is much like a French knife. The style with the long, thin blade is considered to have limited use in the Orient, but is good for slicing and filleting. The cleaver (with rectangular blade) comes in several weights and sizes. A heavy one with thick blade is used for cutting through small bones and mincing. A lighter one with thinner blade is the most widely used "all-purpose" knife in both China and Japan.

Another useful cutting tool is a **Japanese shredder,** which has a selection of blades for shreds of various widths and can be adjusted without the blades to cut paper-thin or thick slices. The **fine grater** sketched is for ginger root or citrus peel.

The **Japanese mortar, suribachi,** consists of a pottery bowl roughly grooved inside and comes with a wooden **pestle.**

An inexpensive bamboo article is the **Japanese sudare,** a flexible mat used for rolling Sushi, rice rolls for which there is a recipe on page 84.

The Chinese use a **curved spatula** and a **long-handled ladle** to stir-fry foods in a wok, but you can make do with a slotted spoon or spatula.

The attractive **wire ladles** sketched on page 20 are useful for deep-frying or for dipping foods from the communal "hot pot." The most useful skimmer of all is the fine-mesh, **screen-wire skimmer.** This type can remove the most tiny bits of food, including those that remain in the oil and burn when you deep-fry. **Bamboo tongs** are handy for removing food from broth, oil, or grill.

FAR-EASTERN DISHES FOR WESTERN TABLES

In many cases the serving dishes used in China, Japan, or Korea are different from each other in shape or decoration. In other cases they are the same, or similar enough to be used interchangeably.

Rather than describing the dishes of these three countries separately, the following paragraphs tell about general types of serving equipment and make useful comparisons. Most of these dishes and tools are sketched on page 21.

Chopsticks and Other Tools. Chinese and Japanese chopsticks are usually different in shape. The **Chinese chopsticks** are longer, less tapered, and with blunt ends for picking up food. The **Japanese chopsticks** are shorter, very tapered, and with pointed ends.

Chopsticks for eating come in a variety of materials—throw-away wood, plain or painted wood, plastic, lacquer, or ivory. Longer chopsticks of wood or metal are for cooking.

Chopstick rests are attractive little gadgets to lay the sticks on when not in use.

The photograph on page 18 shows you how to hold and use chopsticks.

Knives are not provided at Oriental meals because all the foods are cut into bite-sized pieces or are soft enough to tear apart with chopsticks. But spoons or ladles are used for serving. The **ceramic spoon** sketched on page 21 is used for serving or for eating soup which cannot be sipped from the bowl.

Rice-serving paddles of bamboo or lacquer are for serving rice from a big container into individual bowls.

Drink Servers. In all countries **teacups** most often have a small, rounded shape with no handles and usually no saucers. However, some cups, typically Japanese, are more straight-sided and taller (see sketch on page 21).

If you shop around, you will soon see that designs on some cups and **teapots** may be more Chinese in character, while others more Japanese. However, you can find designs and textures which seem typical of both countries.

If you serve wine or beer, you may decide that plain glass tumblers look better than the glasses traditionally used for these beverages in Europe and America. Some people like to use the taller or larger teacups for wine.

If you serve the Japanese rice wine, *sake*, you may like to buy a **sake jug** (with saucer to go underneath) and **small cups.** Several styles are sketched on page 21.

Rice Bowls and Buckets. In all countries each person is served an individual bowl of rice. These bowls have certain shapes which you will come to recognize as different from the bowls used for soup or other purposes. **Chinese and Japanese rice bowls** come with or without covers (see several sketched).

Rice may be brought to the table in the individual bowls, but it is more customary to set the table with the empty bowls and then serve the rice from one large bowl or bucket. You may use an ordinary bowl, or you may buy **lidded rice buckets** of wood or lacquer. A rustic and a more polished style are pictured on page 21.

Both individual and large rice bowls used in Korea and parts of China may be made of metal richly embossed with designs. One style of **Korean metal rice bowl** is sketched.

Soup Bowls and Other Bowls. Soup bowls may come in a variety of shapes, but one type of **Chinese soup bowl** is flat and shallow, as sketched on page 21.

Another style, which all countries may use but which the Japanese prefer, is more rounded. This may come with a cover, and often is made of lacquer. This **Japanese soup bowl** is small enough to hold up while sipping the soup.

Other types of bowls in all the countries come in a variety of shapes and sizes for everything from pickles to soupy main dishes. Most are all-purpose bowls, but a few have been designed for particular dishes. One such dish is the **Japanese meshi donburi** (*donburi* means "bowl") for the foods called Donburi, rice topped with meat, fish, or eggs. This is a rimmed bowl with a cover that resembles a rice or soup bowl, but is larger.

Another special type is the lidded teacup-shaped **Japanese Chawan Mushi dish** for a steamed custard called Chawan Mushi (see recipe on page 76).

Other donburi, about the same size as rice or soup bowls but shaped differently, you will come to recognize as the proper **Japanese bowls for salad-type foods.** The uninitiated might not know that these three types of bowls of similar size have subtle differences in shape and completely different uses.

Plates, Platters, and Serving Dishes. Plates for eating or serving in all the countries may be the ordinary round shape.

But **plates** are made in delightful other shapes, too—rectangular, square, hexagonal, oval, and who-knows-what.

Chinese foods, unless they are soups, may be served on large **platters** or **pedestal dishes** (see sketches on page 21). At most Chinese meals, everyone helps himself from these platters in the center of the table.

In Japan it is more typical for servings of each food to be prepared for each person on individual dishes, often presented on individual lacquer trays. Therefore, you need more small plates for Japanese service.

Baskets or **bamboo steamer trays** may double as plates or platters wherever practical. **Lacquer boxes or trays** are multi-purpose serving utensils. **Lacquer stack boxes** are used by the Japanese for special occasions including New Year's to contain an entire cold meal prepared ahead. **Metal stack boxes** with handles are for picnics or carrying a lunch to work.

Sauce and Pickle Dishes. All the Oriental cuisines are replete with foods which require dipping sauces served on the side. Pickles are very frequently served, too. Many **tiny condiment dishes** in a multitude of shapes are made for these (see sketch on page 21).

Some **soy sauce pitchers** are designed to prevent dripping as you pour. The **teapot-style sauce pitcher** can be used for soy sauce or broth when you cook at the table.

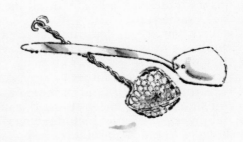

MEAL PLANNING & PARTY MENUS

Tested menus...plus a guide to composing your own

The menus at the end of this chapter mostly are based on large one-dish meals, many cooked at the table, or unique entertaining ideas.

However, you can compose your own menus of individual dishes from recipes in this book. To help you plan, first some basic menu principles are presented in the form of a checklist. Then Chinese and Japanese meal patterns and serving styles are summarized. Use these summaries as guides, but don't be afraid to make changes to suit your style of life.

Korean meal patterns are not summarized because two menus which incorporate nearly all the recipes are on pages 27 and 29. The Korean Banquet menu there will give you a good idea of what a typical large meal is like.

SOME UNIVERSAL TIPS FOR MENU PLANNING

Whether your menu is Chinese, Japanese, or even French, you can consider some basic principles to make sure the meal will be pleasing.

These universal principles follow in the form of a question checklist. After you have composed a menu, run through these questions to see whether you have overlooked some important consideration.

(1) *Do the foods offer contrast in color?* Avoid having dishes which are all pale, or all dark, or all much the same color.

(2) *Is there variety in texture?* Some of the foods should be soft, smooth, or liquid while others should be firm, chewy, or crunchy.

(3) *Is there variety in the main ingredients?* Avoid repeating a certain kind of meat or vegetable. You should avoid using all dried, canned, heavy, or long-cooked foods. Include some which are fresh, crisp, bland, or briefly cooked.

(4) *Is there variety in the sauces or seasonings?* Avoid serving the same kind of sauce with more than one dish. Consider whether dominant flavors of vinegar, garlic, soy sauce, ginger, or other distinctive seasoners are repeated. Some dishes should be pungently seasoned, others bland.

(5) *Is there too much last-minute cooking?* It is especially important that you avoid much work shortly before guests arrive or while they are being served. If you are not experienced at Oriental cooking, you will probably need more time than you think for seemingly easy tasks.

(6) *Have you planned too many dishes, or too many complicated or new dishes?* Keep your first Oriental meals simple. Don't try more than one or two dishes that require cooking techniques new to you. Do everything you can ahead of time and start earlier than you usually would. Many Oriental dishes require much chopping, or various small steps which cannot be hurried. You may not know how to estimate the time necessary and may find yourself in a last-minute dither.

CHINESE MENU & SERVING PATTERNS

In every country on earth there are various ways of dining—from picnics to formal banquets. In large countries, such as China, regional differences also exist.

Nevertheless, there are two main patterns for Chinese meals. These might be called family-style and banquet-style.

At family meals all the dishes, perhaps even soup, are placed in the center of the table in serving platters or bowls—at the same time. Rice bowls and small plates may be provided for each person. But, each person eats out of the serving dishes with his chopsticks. This pattern is followed at many Chinese restaurants in America for small or large groups, although sometimes the soup is served first (a Cantonese custom) and spoons are provided so that individual portions can be dished out.

If you are not experienced at Chinese cooking, serving a family-style meal may be difficult. You must prepare everything so it will be ready at the same time and then make sure everyone is seated promptly.

You may prefer to serve banquet-style—in courses—even if your meals are very simple. A banquet begins with small cold dishes or appetizers already on the table. Then hot dishes are served one by one. The most special or heavy foods come near the end. Sweet-and-sour dishes may be served last. Rice is served at the end, if at all (it is not a necessity at a banquet). Several soups may appear at various points during the meal, the middle and the end usually. (Oddly, sweets comparable to dessert may be served after this "middle" soup.)

Adjust the way you serve to suit yourself. It is better to present the food well prepared, fresh, and piping hot—whenever you can manage it—than to chose a meal pattern which you cannot accomplish with ease and grace.

Don't try to prepare more than a few dishes until you are experienced at Chinese cooking. A soup (usually prepared ahead) and two or three main dishes will be sufficient. Try to select recipes which have different main ingredients, such as one chicken, one beef, and one shrimp dish. Also consider the sauces, seasonings, and overall predominant flavors; don't duplicate them.

Another important aspect to vary is the method of cooking these main dishes. You might, for example, plan one roasted duck dish, one steamed fish dish, and one stir-fried chicken-and-vegetable dish. This plan not only lends variety, but also automatically prevents too much last-minute work.

Variety is the most essential spice used in the Chinese cuisine, a spice you cannot add too liberally.

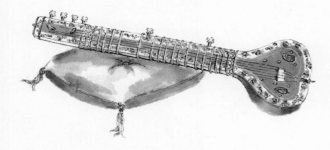

JAPANESE MENU & SERVING PATTERNS

At Chinese meals, the foods are presented in large serving dishes from which each person takes a portion. Most Japanese meals are completely different.

Practically every food is arranged ahead of time on individual dishes for each person, or an empty individual dish may be provided into which the hostess will serve foods prepared at the table or brought to the table in a large pot or on a tray.

Additionally, each person's meal may be arranged on an individual tray, or even a series of trays for banquets. If trays are not used, each person's individual dishes are placed before him much as they would have been arranged on the individual tray.

Several types of foods may be served at most meals, whether simple or elaborate: rice; pickles, *tsukemono*; and soup, either clear soup called *suimono* or made with *miso* bean paste and called *misoshiru*. Rice may be omitted if rice or noodles are an important part of a main dish.

To these basic foods a large or small selection of other foods may be added. Classifications have been developed for these types of foods. A menu probably would not include more than one dish from each classification. Various rules have been devised for where servings of these types of foods are placed on the individual trays and for the order in which they are eaten (hot foods first usually).

Most of the main classifications are these: broiled foods, *yakimono*; boiled foods, *nimono*; steamed foods, *mushimono*; fried, *agemono*; vinegared foods, *sunomono*; cold, dressed, salad-like foods, *aemono*; broiled greens, *hitashimono*; rice with other ingredients, *meshimono*; sliced raw fish, *sashimi*; and appetizers, *zensai*.

Other classifications exist for foods which usually comprise a whole meal: seasoned cold rice with various other ingredients, *sushi*; saucepan foods, *nabemono*, usually cooked in the presence of the diners (Sukiyaki is an example); and batter-fried foods known as *tempura*.

Smaller "full-meal" dishes may have rice or noodles as a base. *Donburi* dishes consist of rice in a bowl topped with protein or vegetable ingredients. Noodle dishes named according to the type of noodle (*udon*, *somen*, or *soba*) also may be topped with various foods to make a balanced light meal.

These classifications may be somewhat confusing, but knowing about them will help you to understand Japanese cuisine.

(Continued on next page)

However, it will be much easier to plan menus from recipes in this book if you *ignore* the classic categories and proceed this way:

Many of the recipes are for "full-meal" dishes. Just add rice, soup, pickles, tea, and—if you like, simple appetizers and a fruit dessert.

If you want a more elaborate meal of individual dishes, still include the rice, soup, pickles, and tea. Then select one or two main dishes prepared different ways with different seasonings. Choose a cold dish that resembles a salad, no matter what its Japanese classification would be or whether it is vegetable or protein. If you like, start with a selection of appetizers and end with dessert.

Don't worry about including more than one dish containing seafood. Seafood is so important in Japan that it often appears in two or three forms at a large meal.

If you plan a menu that would be well balanced by American standards, you probably will accidentally hit upon a pleasing Japanese menu. If not, you will at least please yourself and those you serve—much more important than strict authenticity.

ORIENTAL PARTY MENUS TO SUIT WESTERN LIFE

Most of the menus on the following pages feature well-known dishes which Americans like readily. They also are designed for easy preparation by beginners at Oriental cookery.

Japanese Tempura Party

If the weather is warm enough for you to entertain outside, you can set up a sturdy table on the patio or beside the pool and deep-fry Tempura to order for your guests over a brazier or in an electric pan.

If you must be indoors, it is better to do the cooking in the kitchen where odors and splatters of oil or batter will not be a problem. If you don't want to be away from guests long, save this party idea for summertime.

Tempura-making is photographed on page 31.

SEAFOOD-VEGETABLE TEMPURA
Recipe on page 81

COLD BEER OR FRUIT PUNCHES

The Tempura recipe provides an assortment of seafoods and vegetables which are batter-coated and fried in oil until crisp. The batter recipe is enough to coat foods for a main dish serving 4 to 6 people, or for appetizers serving about 12 people.

Guests can pick up the Tempura and eat out of hand (provide plenty of napkins). Prepare the dipping sauce with the recipe only if you like. Lemon wedges and salt would be sufficient and neater.

Peking Duck Dinner

Very little about this meal is strictly authentic. True Peking duck is a complicated dish to prepare, but this simplified version captures the savor and flavor. The Thousand-Layer Buns are made from refrigerated biscuits, which save time without as much loss in quality as you might think. The romaine salad and dessert are Americanized additions, but very compatible.

HOT CHICKEN BROTH
Season broth with a dash of soy sauce

WESTERN-STYLE PEKING DUCK
Recipe on page 51

CONDIMENTS: SLICED GREEN ONIONS, CHINESE PLUM SAUCE, AND CHOPPED CHINESE PARSLEY
Information follows

QUICK THOUSAND-LAYER BUNS
Recipe on page 63

SPEARS OF ROMAINE
Serve with salt to eat like celery

COUPES CHINOISE
Instructions follow

The recipe calls for two ducks, enough for 4 persons. Serve half a duck to each person, with a knife, to carve as desired.

To eat, place meat and skin on a bun, top with condiments, and fold bun around filling. Eat out of hand. Pick up the romaine to eat also.

Shopping information about the plum sauce is on page 12, and about the Chinese parsley on page 11.

To make the coupes for dessert, place a scoop of vanilla ice cream on sliced oranges, garnish with bottled preserved kumquats (sliced if you prefer), and drizzle with an orange-flavored liqueur such as Cointreau or Triple Sec. A recipe for preserving kumquats is on page 66.

Japanese Kabuto Yaki

This is a meal of meat and vegetable tidbits barbecued over charcoal, best reserved for mild weather when you can be out of doors. The traditional barbecue is the domed Genghis Khan grill described on page 22. But you can use any barbecue if you cover the grill with "expanded steel," welded hardware cloth, or broiler rack so that the food won't fall through.

The party is photographed on page 31.

CLEAR SOUP OR CHICKEN BROTH
Clear Soup recipe on page 73

CUCUMBER SUNOMONO
Recipe on page 71

KABUTO YAKI WITH GOMA (SESAME) SAUCE
Recipe on page 78

STEAMED RICE
Recipe on page 83

WATERMELON FOR DESSERT

BEER OR TEA

The soup, cucumber dish which serves as a salad, and rice may be placed in individual dishes on a tray for each person. To each tray, add chopsticks, napkin, teacup, a small dish containing the Goma Sauce, and a plate with uncooked meat and vegetables.

Provide forks or cooking chopsticks for each person to remove his portions of meat and vegetables from the barbecue. Recipe serves 6 persons, but is easily doubled.

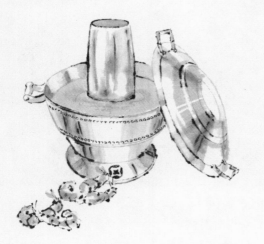

Korean Banquet

This meal lets you sample many typical Korean dishes, some flavored with the crushed sesame and chiles typical of this spicy cuisine. Although this is an elaborate meal, most of the dishes can be completely or partially cooked ahead.

BEEF BARBECUE APPETIZERS
Recipe on page 89

DUMPLING SOUP
Recipe on page 91

BRAISED CHICKEN
Recipe on page 92

WATERCRESS SALAD
Recipe on page 91

SKEWERED BEEF AND MUSHROOMS
Recipe on page 92

CABBAGE PICKLES (KIM CHEE)
Recipe on page 92

RICE
Recipes on pages 60 or 83

APPLES AND ORANGES FOR DESSERT

You can buy the cabbage pickles, Kim Chee, and Won Ton wrappers for the soup if you have access to an Oriental market and want to save time, but recipes for both are in this book.

The meal will serve 4 hearty eaters, or 6 if you double the skewered beef recipe.

Chinese "Hot Pot" Dinner

Too many cooks don't spoil the broth in the bubbling Chinese "hot pot." Everyone sitting around the table helps flavor the broth by cooking his own meal in it.

You may seat four to six "cooks" together around a small table or two groups at either end of a longer dining table. Each group shares a pot of bubbling chicken broth in which each person cooks his own meat, fish, chicken, and vegetables. The pot may be the Oriental "hot pot" especially made for this meal, but an electric frying pan works very well. (See Cook-at-the-Table Equipment on page 19 for complete details.)

Also see photograph on next page.

Toward the end of the meal, the hostess adds

FOUR DIFFERENT POTS FOR COOKING AT THE TABLE

ANCIENT "HOT POT" is heated with charcoal, may be used for several menus, including one on page 27.

CHRYSANTHEMUM BOWL (menu on page 30) may be cooked in a casserole set over an alcohol burner.

JAPANESE MIZUTAKI (menu on page 30) is prepared in an enamel pan over modern-design alcohol burner.

WON TON (recipe on page 34) are deep-fried in electric pan, also good for dishes cooked in broth.

cooked noodles or rice to the broth, which is by now well seasoned, to make a soup.

SLICED MEATS, SEAFOOD, AND VEGETABLES
"Hot Pot" recipe on page 58

SAUCES FOR DIPPING COOKED FOODS
With "Hot Pot" recipe

CHICKEN-NOODLE OR RICE SOUP
Prepared at the table

FORTUNE COOKIES OR ALMOND COOKIES
Almond cookie recipe on page 66

CHINESE TEA
Instructions on page 67

Each place setting should have a plate for eating (salad size is best if the table is small) and, if you choose, a plate of raw foods.

For cooking, give each person a wire ladle or a large slotted spoon. Those who know how to manipulate chopsticks well may use the metal or unfinished wooden ones for cooking. Provide small individual dishes for sauces. Several types of wire ladles and spoons, and sauce dishes are sketched on page 20 and 21.

Mandarin Pancake Dinner

The Mandarin pancake is a north Chinese version of a sandwich. The recipes here will serve 4 hearty eaters without much strain on a cook, even one unaccustomed to cooking Oriental food.

STEAMED MANDARIN PANCAKES
Recipe on page 63

FILLINGS: BEEF WITH HOT CHILE
CHICKEN WITH BEAN SPROUTS
EGGS WITH SCALLOPS
Recipe on page 59

SAUCE SUGGESTIONS
With filling recipes on page 60

CANNED LITCHIS
Information about litchis on page 16

The chicken and the beef fillings can be assembled ready to cook, then chilled; the scallops for the egg dish can also be cooked ahead and kept cold. Quickly cook the beef and chicken while the pancakes are steaming; each takes less than

5 minutes. Prepare the eggs just before serving.

Each person fills a hot pancake with one of the fillings, dabs on a sauce, and rolls up the pancake, folding the bottom end over to hold contents in. However, this preventive measure doesn't always succeed. Provide large napkins to tuck in the neck bib-fashion.

Korean Sin Sul Lo

Sin Sul Lo is a complete-meal dish cooked at the table in a "hot pot" or similar vessel, just as are the Chinese Chrysanthemum Bowl, "Hot Pot," and Japanese Mizutaki dishes also featured in menus here.

This Korean version is more simple because you arrange the foods in the pot in the kitchen and just finish the cooking at the table. No sauces are served.

As with all such dishes, you serve the well-flavored cooking broth as a soup after the main dish has been eaten.

See the section on Cook-at-the-Table Equipment for full information about the "hot pot" and substitute equipment, page 19.

CABBAGE PICKLES
Called Kim Chee, buy or make by recipe on page 92

SIN SUL LO OF BEEF, PORK BALLS, AND VEGETABLES
Recipe on page 90

SOUP OF BROTH FROM THE COOKING POT

STEAMED RICE
Recipes on pages 60 or 83

GREEN TEA
Instructions on page 88

DESSERT OF ORANGES OR PERSIMMONS
Or other fruit in season

At each place set a small plate, rice bowl, teacup, a cup or soup bowl for drinking the cooking broth at the conclusion of the meal, chopsticks, fork, and a napkin.

Serve the rice and tea throughout the meal or near the end, as you prefer.

You can prepare and cook the ingredients for Sin Sul Lo several hours ahead. Arrange the food in the cooker shortly before you serve it. The recipe is sufficient for 4 to 6 people.

Japanese Sukiyaki

Prepare the Sukiyaki at the table in the special Sukiyaki pan sketched on page 20 or in a suitable substitute described in the section on Cook-at-the-Table equipment on page 19.

JAPANESE PICKLES
See suggestions for pickles to buy on page 69

MISO SOUP
Recipe on page 74

SUKIYAKI
Recipe on page 80

STEAMED RICE
Recipe on page 83

WARM SAKE (RICE WINE)
Heating instructions on page 88

GREEN TEA
Instructions on page 88

CHILLED CANNED MANDARIN ORANGES

Serve the pickles in tiny dishes for each person. Prepare the soup ahead and reheat at serving time; serve in individual bowls.

Cut and arrange the uncooked foods for Sukiyaki an hour or two ahead, cover, and refrigerate. The Sukiyaki recipe serves 4.

Serve sake throughout the meal and the tea at the end.

Chinese Chrysanthemum Bowl Dinner

This is one of the dishes cooked at the table in a "hot pot" filled with broth. See section called Cook-at-the-Table Equipment for details about the pot and how to fire it, as well as for information on substitute equipment (page 19).

Preparation of the Chrysanthemum Bowl comes to a dramatic conclusion as the hostess plucks chrysanthemum blossoms and sprinkles them as flavoring into the rich broth left after meat, seafood, and vegetables have been cooked. This ceremony is photographed on page 28.

Set each place with a small plate, chopsticks, fork, napkin, rice bowl, teacup, a soup bowl for drinking the broth, and one of the raw eggs mentioned in the recipe (which each guest will cook in the broth). Also include tiny dishes for the

condiments, if you use them. Near the "hot pot," place a ladle, a slotted spoon, and the blossoms.

CHRYSANTHEMUM BOWL
Recipe on page 57

STEAMED RICE
Recipe on page 60

CANDIED COCONUT, PRESERVED GINGER, CANDIED FRUITS AND CITRUS PEEL, FORTUNE COOKIES

GREEN TEA
Instructions on page 88

Prepare the main dish according to the recipe which will serve 6 people. Provide rice and tea throughout the meal. For dessert, pass a plate of the candied fruits and cookies.

Japanese Mizutaki Dinner

This meal cooked at the table in a communal pot originated with water as the cooking liquid (*mizu means water*). But here broth is used.

For full information about the pot to use, see Cook-at-the-Table Equipment on page 19. Also see dinner photograph on page 28.

APPETIZERS YOU CAN BUY
See suggestions on page 68

MIZUTAKI DINNER
Recipe on page 79

DIPPING SAUCES FOR MIZUTAKI
Choice of two sauces with Mizutaki Dinner recipe

STEAMED RICE
Recipe on page 83

FRUIT COMPOTE
Instructions follow

GREEN TEA
Instructions on page 88

The Mizutaki Dinner recipe, which serves 6 people, gives you information about how to set the table and procedure for cooking the food.

To provide a dessert compote to please Americans, you can combine canned mandarin oranges and pineapple chunks with some of their juices. If you like, garnish with slivers of preserved or candied ginger, described on page 11.

KABUTO YAKI, a meal of broiled meats and vegetables, is prepared on a domed Genghis Khan grill. Guests cook own foods, then dip them in a sauce. A menu featuring Kabuto Yaki is on page 27.

JAPANESE TEMPURA (menu on page 26) is batter-coated seafood and vegetables deep-fried by the hostess. It's excellent food for party held when weather is warm enough for cooking out of doors.

A CHINESE RECIPE SAMPLER

A few of the infinite dishes from an enormous land

Useful information has been included in chapters at the front of this book to help you cook and serve the recipes here.

For a quick survey of principles which apply to all Oriental cooking, read The Essence of an Oriental Art on page 4.

Whenever an unusual ingredient is specified in a recipe, it will be followed with the words "description on page ....." This refers you to the Ingredient Shopping Guide beginning on page 8. There you will find a thorough description of the ingredient and information about where to buy it.

You don't need special equipment for cooking and serving Oriental food. But items you might buy for pleasure are described in Tools and Utensils, How to Use Them, beginning on page 17.

General information about planning meals from these recipes and specific menus based on them are in the chapter called Meal Planning and Party Menus beginning on page 24.

APPETIZERS & "DOT HEART" SNACKS

Chinese appetizers are filling, and the "Dot Heart" snacks (see right) enough for a meal.

Appetizers You Can Buy

To save yourself work, you can buy several foods for appetizers.

At Chinese shops you can find toasted, salted melon seed, sometimes glazed with soy sauce, to serve like nuts. Or serve salted almonds.

At Chinese meat shops, you can buy barbecued pork (*chahr siu*) which you just slice evenly and serve cold, with a dip of chile sauce or hot mustard sauce described on page 12.

Canned abalone may just be sliced and served

on skewers, plain or with a soy sauce dip.

At many supermarkets you can find puffy, pastel shrimp chips ready to eat, sold in bags along with the potato chips. At Oriental stores, you can buy them uncooked in the form of hard, translucent discs—ask for shrimp chips. Just drop a few discs at a time in 2 inches of salad oil heated to 365°. They will puff immediately; remove at once and drain on paper towels. Serve hot or cold, salted lightly if you like.

"Dot-Heart" Lunch

A pleasant substitute for lunch, or even dinner on a warm evening, is the Cantonese high tea known in Hong Kong as *yum cha*. Tea is served with a tremendous variety of small tidbits passed around on a tray for your selection. Hot meat-and-vegetable dishes and soups may be served, but the main attraction is a group of dishes called *deem sum*. Deem sum means "touch the heart" or "dot heart" and implies a snack or appetizer.

Several recipes here are for treats which are typically deem sum, or similar. These are: Steamed Buns, page 37; Shrimp Dumplings, 35; Pork Dumplings, 35; Barbecued Pork, 33; Filled Fresh "Rice" Noodles, 38; Egg Rolls, 34; and Fried Won Ton, 34.

You can also serve simple noodle dishes such as the Noodles in Sauce, page 61.

Sweet things are included, too. One recipe in the dessert section is a deem sum: Sweet Bean Buns, page 66.

At Chinese pastry shops and some restaurants you can buy many of these things "to go."

Spiced Chicken Livers

No appetizer could be easier to make than this one you can prepare as much as a day ahead.

    1   pound chicken livers
        Water
    ½   cup each soy sauce and chopped green onions,
            including tops
    ¼   cup dry vermouth, sherry, or white rice wine
            (sake, described on page 10)
    1   tablespoon sugar
    ¼   teaspoon anise seed
    1½ teaspoons chopped fresh ginger root, or
            ⅜ teaspoon ground ginger

Cover livers with water and bring just to boiling. Drain well. Add soy sauce, green onions, wine, sugar, anise seed, and ginger. Bring to boiling and simmer gently, covered, for 15 minutes.

Chill thoroughly in stock. Slice livers in bite-sized pieces, return to stock, keep cold. Drain to serve, at room temperature. Makes about 2 dozen.

Barbecued Pork

This cold, sliced pork is served by many restaurants with a dip of hot mustard sauce or chile sauce to be mixed with soy sauce. It also is used in recipes, such as Steamed Buns on page 37.

You can buy it, too, if you have access to a Chinese meat shop. For shopping instructions, see page 12.

    2   pounds pork butt
    1   clove garlic, minced or mashed
        About ¼-inch slice fresh ginger root, mashed
    2   teaspoons sugar
    1   teaspoon salt
    2   teaspoons sherry
    3   tablespoons soy sauce
    2   tablespoons honey
    ½   teaspoon "five-spice" (description on page 11)
    ½   teaspoon red food coloring

Ask the meat man to bone the meat and cut it into ½ to ¾-inch strips. Combine the garlic, ginger root, sugar, salt, sherry, soy sauce, honey, five-spice, and food coloring. Pour over the meat and marinate for 1 hour.

Remove meat from marinade and roast in a 325° oven for 1½ hours, basting frequently with the marinade and drippings. Makes 8 to 12 appetizer servings.

Sweet & Sour Spareribs

These appetizers can be made ahead. Provide forks or chopsticks for eating.

    1½ pounds spareribs
        Soy sauce
        Sherry
    1   teaspoon minced garlic
        Sugar
        Cornstarch
    1   tablespoon vinegar
        Salad oil

Have your meatman cut crosswise through the bones of the spareribs at about 1½-inch intervals. Cut bones apart.

Combine 3 tablespoons soy sauce, 1 tablespoon sherry, the garlic, and 1 teaspoon sugar; blend with meat. Let stand at room temperature for at least 30 minutes, stirring occasionally. Then blend in 1 tablespoon cornstarch.

Meanwhile, in a pan blend 2 tablespoons *each* sugar and soy sauce, 1 tablespoon sherry, the vinegar, and 1 teaspoon cornstarch. Cook, stirring, until thickened; set aside.

Heat 2 or 3 inches of salad oil in a deep pan to 360°. Drain marinade from spareribs and discard. Add about ¼ of the meat at a time to hot oil and cook 3 to 4 minutes or until very well browned; drain on paper towels. Oil temperature should be at 360° before each addition of meat.

Drop cooked spareribs into the prepared sauce and mix well. Chill, covered. Serve at room temperature. Makes about 2 dozen pieces.

Egg Rolls

Some egg rolls have a crisp and delicate crust, while others have a coating with considerable substance. The difference is that several different "skins" or pancake-type wrappings can be used. The following wrapping is thin and fragile.

At some Chinese stores, you can buy fresh or frozen "wrappers" if you don't want to make your own.

Egg roll fillings also vary considerably. This one contains both pork and shrimp.

1½ cups unsifted regular all-purpose flour
1½ cups cold water
    Salad oil
    Filling (recipe follows)

Mix together flour and cold water until smooth. Have a 10-inch frying pan, some salad oil, and a pastry brush at hand.

Heat the pan over low heat; it must not get too hot. Lightly grease the pan with a crumpled paper towel dipped in salad oil. Then quickly brush on a layer of the batter, in approximately a 5-inch square. If holes appear, brush over some more batter but brush in the opposite direction. Within a half minute or so, the batter will dry into a thin skin. Remove it with a spatula wiped with oil and place on wax paper.

Continue until the batter is all used. To keep them from drying out, cover with a damp-dry towel. The skins will freeze nicely if stacked with wax paper between the pieces and then tightly wrapped, but be careful to thaw thoroughly before trying to roll them.

To make rolls, arrange 1 tablespoon of the filling in a sausage shape along one side of skin. Fold over ends of skin and roll. *See photograph on page 36.*

Paste the roll together with a little water or the flour batter. If skins are so dry you can't roll them easily, brush a little warm water over the edges.

Fry in hot deep fat (370°) until skin is crisp, bubbly, and brown, about 8 to 10 minutes. Cut each roll in 3 or 4 pieces and serve as an appetizer. Makes about 36 rolls.

Filling. Finely chop 1 pound raw pork, 1 pound shelled raw shrimp, and 6 or 8 green onions. Cook them in 1 tablespoon oil for 3 minutes. Add 1 cup chopped bean sprouts, ½ cup finely chopped water chestnuts, 1 tablespoon grated fresh ginger root or 1 tablespoon finely chopped candied ginger (place in strainer and wash off sugar), and 1½ tablespoons soy sauce.

Fried Won Ton

You may buy the 3-inch squares of thin won ton noodles, fresh, cut, wrapped, and refrigerated or frozen at Oriental shops. Or make them from the recipe on page 62.

Serve these filled fried ones for an appetizer, with a mixture of chile sauce and hot mustard sauce made by blending dry (ground) yellow mustard with water to a paste. Or provide a dip of Sweet-and-Sour Sauce, recipe on page 44.

For an entrée, arrange the Fried Won Ton in hot Sweet-and-Sour Sauce on a platter. You can also make soup from these, by simmering them in broth like dumplings rather than frying. The soup recipe is on page 40.

6 dozen won ton noodles
    Shrimp Filling (recipe follows)
    Salad oil for deep frying

Prepare Shrimp Filling and spoon ½ teaspoon into the center of each won ton noodle.

Fold each noodle in half to form a triangle; press around the mound of filling to seal it in place. Form each into a smaller triangle by bringing together the two points at the end of the folded side and overlapping (not just pinching) the folded edge of the skin; moisten inside so the edges will stick together.

Cover the filled Won Ton with clear plastic film or foil and refrigerate until serving time. To fry, heat salad oil in an electric saucepan or deep fat fryer to about 360°. Drop in about ½ dozen at a time; cook, stirring, for a minute or two, until golden brown. Lift out with a slotted spoon and drain on paper towels. *(See photograph on page 28.)* Serve hot or at room temperature. Makes 6 dozen.

Shrimp Filling. Combine ½ pound raw shrimp, peeled and finely chopped, with 2 finely chopped green onions; 2 tablespoons minced parsley; 6 canned water chestnuts, chopped (optional); 1 tablespoon *each* soy sauce and salad oil; 1 teaspoon cornstarch; ¼ teaspoon salt; and ⅛ teaspoon pepper.

Pork Dumplings

The Chinese name for these is *Fin Kue*. You can serve them as appetizers or in the Dumpling Soup, recipe on page 40.

They also can be a part of the "Dot-Heart" Lunch described on page 32.

  2 cups (about 1 lb.) ground lean pork
 ½ cup minced soaked dried mushrooms (directions follow), or ½ cup minced fresh mushrooms
 ⅓ cup minced green onion
 ¼ cup each minced celery, canned water chestnuts, and canned bamboo shoots
  2 teaspoons minced fresh Chinese parsley (described on page 11), or ½ teaspoon ground coriander
  1 teaspoon grated fresh ginger root, or ¼ teaspoon ground ginger
  3 tablespoons soy sauce
1½ tablespoons cornstarch
  1 egg white
    Dumpling Dough (recipe with Shrimp Dumplings on page 37)
 48 fresh or frozen green peas (optional)
    Salad oil

Mix the pork with mushrooms, onion, celery, water chestnuts, bamboo shoots, parsley or coriander, and ginger. Gradually blend soy sauce with cornstarch and add to pork mixture along with the egg white. Beat to blend thoroughly. (At this point you can chill, covered, overnight.) Divide mixture in 48 equal-sized balls.

To make each dumpling, roll a piece of Dumpling Dough out on a very lightly floured board to make a 3-inch-diameter round. Place a pork ball onto the center of the dough. Crumple the dough up and around the filling; the top surface of the filling stays exposed. *See photograph on the next page.*

Put 1 pea in the center of each dumpling, if you like. Brush dumplings all over with salad oil. Keep covered and cold until all are shaped.

To steam, follow directions for Shrimp Dumplings, and cook for a total of 20 minutes. You can serve, or reheat and serve, or freeze as directed for Shrimp Dumplings. Makes about 48 dumplings.

Soaked Dried Mushrooms. Cover 4 large dried mushrooms with ½ cup warm water mixed with 1 teaspoon sugar. Soak at least 30 minutes. Drain, rinse, and squeeze dry. Discard stems and mince caps to make ½ cup. Shopping information about the mushrooms is on page 16.

Shrimp Dumplings

The Chinese name for these is *Har Gow*. You can serve them as appetizers or in the Dumpling Soup, recipe on page 40.

They also can be a part of the "Dot-Heart" Lunch described on page 32.

1¾ pounds medium-sized raw shrimp, shelled and deveined
 ⅔ cup minced canned bamboo shoots
  1 teaspoon grated fresh ginger root, or ¼ teaspoon ground ginger
  1 teaspoon minced fresh Chinese parsley (described on page 11, or ¼ teaspoon ground coriander
 ¼ cup minced pork fat
 ⅛ teaspoon anise seed, crushed
 ⅛ teaspoon white pepper
  1 teaspoon salt
    Dumpling Dough (recipe follows)
    Salad oil

Grind shrimp through medium blade of a food chopper and measure exactly 2 cups. Mix shrimp with bamboo shoots, ginger, parsley or coriander, pork fat, anise seed, pepper, and salt. (You can chill mixture, covered, overnight.) Divide shrimp mixture into 30 equal-sized portions.

To make each dumpling, roll a piece of the Dumpling Dough out on a moderately floured board to make a round 4 to 4½ inches in diameter. Spoon a single portion of the shrimp filling down the center of the dough round. Lift opposite sides of the round over the filling and pinch together, fluting to seal in filling completely. *See these half-moon-shaped dumplings in photograph on the next page.*

Brush the entire surface of each dumpling generously with salad oil. Keep covered and cold until all are shaped.

Cover a wire or perforated steamer rack with foil and brush foil with salad oil. See information on steamers you can buy or improvise and how to use them on page 19.

Place rack in a steamer or deep pan, keeping rack several inches above water level. Perforate the foil liberally with a fork to prevent the accumulation of moisture while cooking. The pan should be deep enough to allow a lid to cover dumplings without touching. Have 2 or 3 inches of water boiling in pan and keep at a steady boil.

To steam dumplings, place slightly apart on rack, cover, and cook 15 minutes. Serve at once.

Or you can reheat for hot appetizers in the steamer for about 5 minutes. (If you cook dumplings ahead, keep cold and covered for no longer

HOW TO SHAPE THREE "DOT-HEART" SNACKS

STEAMED BUNS are made by wrapping circles of dough around a meat filling and pinching to seal. Buns are decorated with dots of food coloring, then steamed. Bun recipe is on opposite page.

EGG ROLLS (recipe on page 34) are made from pancake-like "skins" wrapped around filling this way.

DUMPLINGS being formed contain pork, and the half-moon ones contain shrimp (recipes on page 35).

than 1 day.) Provide a dip of soy sauce or hot mustard sauce made by blending dry mustard with water to paste consistency.

If you serve the dumplings in soup, just reheat them in the hot soup.

You can also freeze the cooked dumplings for up to 1 month; place slightly apart on a sheet of waxed paper on a baking sheet and freeze until firm, then store in plastic freezer bags. Remove from bags and set dumplings apart to thaw; if they touch, the dough skins stick together. Reheat as directed above. Makes 30 dumplings.

Dumpling Dough. Stir ½ cup boiling water into 1 cup unsifted all-purpose flour, blending thoroughly with a fork or chopsticks. Use this amount of flour and water to make dough for Shrimp Dumplings or for Pork Dumplings on page 35.

Double this amount to make *both* kinds at once.

Knead on moderately floured board for 10 minutes, or until very smooth and velvety. Cover for 20 minutes.

To make Shrimp Dumplings, roll dough into a 15-inch-long log. Cut in 1-inch sections and then cut each section in half to make 30 pieces. Keep covered with clear plastic film at all times.

To make Pork Dumplings, roll dough into a log 24 inches long and cut in 1-inch lengths, then cut each section in half to make 48 pieces. Keep covered with plastic.

Do not divide the log of dough into sections until you are ready to fill dumplings.

Steamed Buns

Steamed buns called *Bow* are savory yeast-dough pastries with round shape, smooth white skin, meat filling, and often a red dot or swirl on top.

These are easy to make at home, very pleasing to American tastes, and practical because the buns freeze well. They make good appetizers or a meal if you combine them with a hot meat-and-vegetable dish.

Or, they also can be a part of the "Dot-Heart" Lunch described on page 32.

1 package (about 14 oz.) hot roll mix
  Choice of meat fillings (recipes follow)
  Red food coloring (optional)
  Dry mustard
  Soy sauce

A photograph showing the buns being made is on the opposite page.

Prepare roll mix and let rise the first time as directed on the package. Punch down the risen dough and knead gently on a lightly floured board just until smooth. Pinch off pieces of dough that are between walnut and egg size.

On a lightly floured board, pat or roll out the pieces of dough to 3-inch rounds. With floured finger tips, press outside edges of dough to make them slightly thinner than the rest of the round (so edges pinched together will not be thick with dough).

Spoon 1 to 2 tablespoons of filling in center of each round. Pull edges up around filling and pinch together to seal in. Place each bun, pinched side down, on a 3-inch square of foil. Allow to rise in a warm place for about 15 minutes or until about doubled in size. Place buns 1 inch apart on a perforated steamer tray. Set in steamer over boiling water. For information about steamers to buy or improvise and how to use, see page 19.

Cover and steam, without lifting the lid, for 12 to 15 minutes. (When perfectly done, tops of buns should be glazed and smooth; if they've begun to wrinkle, they have been steamed a little too long.)

A red dot or any other marking on top of the buns you buy indicates the kind of filling inside. We suggest that you adopt this system to tell the buns apart if you make more than one kind. Dip the tip of a chopstick or skewer into undiluted food coloring and touch it to the top of the buns, either as you form them or after they have been steamed. It is better to add color after steaming, as the steam may cause the color to run.

To freeze the buns, steam them as directed. When cooled, wrap and freeze. To serve, put the frozen buns, on their foil, into a steamer. Resteam just until heated through, about 15 minutes.

When you serve them, offer a little dish of dry ground yellow mustard, blended to a paste with soy sauce. The buns are dipped in this as they are eaten. Makes 16 to 18 buns.

Sausage Filling. Either freeze Chinese pork sausages for about a week or parboil about 15 minutes before using. Remove the strings attached and finely slice or chop about 6 to fill about 18 rolls. A description of the sausages called *lop cheong* is on page 12.

Barbecued Pork Filling. You'll need about 1½ cups of finely chopped barbecued pork for 18 buns. You can buy the pork already cooked (description on page 12) or make it from the recipe on page 33.

Filled Fresh "Rice" Noodles

Similar fresh noodles you can buy at Chinese shops (called *fun*) are made of rice flour. At home, cooks often use cake flour because it is easier to work with, more available, and gives identical results.

Serve cold as an appetizer or include in the "Dot-Heart" Lunch described on page 32.

    ½ cup unsifted cake flour
    ¼ teaspoon salt
    1 cup water
    ¼ cup minced green onion, including tops (optional)
       Salad oil
       Filling (directions follow)
       Soy sauce

Measure flour and salt into a small bowl and gradually blend in water, mixing until smooth. Stir in the onions if you like.

Choose a deep saucepan that is wide enough across to let you nest a 9-inch pie pan in the top of it. Fill the big pan about half full with water; bring to a boil. Lightly grease a 9-inch pie pan with salad oil (you'll need 2 or 3 of these pans) and pour in about 3 tablespoons flour mixture; tilt to distribute batter evenly.

Set filled pie pan level on top of pan of boiling water and cover loosely with waxed paper. Cook 4 minutes or until noodle is firm. Remove from heat and let cool. Run blade of a knife around edge of noodle and gently peel out of pan, taking care not to tear. Repeat procedure until batter is all used.

Cover noodles and keep cool until ready to use (within the day). Distribute about ⅓ cup cold filling over each and roll up like a jelly roll. Cut each in about 1½-inch-long sections and serve cold with soy sauce dip. Makes 5 or 6 noodles, or about 36 sections.

Filling. Heat 2 tablespoons salad oil over high heat in a wide frying pan. Add 1½ cups very thinly slivered cooked ham or Canadian bacon, 4 teaspoons soy sauce, 2 teaspoons brown sugar; cook rapidly, stirring until liquid has evaporated. Stir in 1 cup well-drained parboiled or canned bean sprouts, ½ cup chopped water chestnuts, and 1 tablespoon minced fresh parsley or Chinese parsley (described on page 11).

SOUPS, SIMPLE OR HEARTY MAIN-DISH

Soups are seldom light, but substantial enough to count as a main dish.

Watercress Soup

Simple as it is, this soup is considered extremely nutritious. An elderly Chinese man in Honolulu was told he had only a few days to live by his American doctor. He demanded watercress soup three times a day, and four days later he was hale and hearty once more.

    2 cans (about 14 oz. each) regular-strength
         chicken broth
    ¼ teaspoon salt
    ¾ teaspoon sugar
    2 teaspoons soy sauce
    2 to 4 paper-thin slices fresh ginger root
    ½ cup water
    1 large bunch watercress, stems removed and
         broken into sprigs
    2 tablespoons finely sliced green onions

In a saucepan, combine the chicken broth, salt, sugar, soy sauce, ginger, and water. Simmer for about 15 minutes.

Then bring to a full boil and add watercress and green onions. Cover, reduce heat, and simmer 2 minutes. Serve at once to 4 to 6.

Mustard Greens and Mushroom Variation. Instead of watercress, use 1 bunch regular mustard greens or 1 head mustard cabbage, described on page 15.

Discard stems and tough outer leaves of regular mustard; break leaves into bite-sized pieces. Or, break leaves of mustard cabbage into bite-sized pieces and thinly slice the tender stems.

Wash 4 large dried mushrooms, described on page 16.

Soak mushrooms 30 minutes in the ½ cup water (warm) mentioned in the recipe. Reserve soaking liquid and slice mushrooms into ¼-inch strips, discarding stems.

When you prepare the chicken broth, include the soaking liquid, add mushroom strips, and increase simmering time to 25 minutes.

Then, add mustard leaves (and sliced stems if used); simmer 3 minutes. Add green onions, and simmer 2 minutes more.

Fuzzy Melon Chicken Soup

If you can find the fuzzy melon, then this soup is easy to make.

A picture of the melon is shown with other vegetables on page 13.

- 2 pieces (each about 1½ inches in diameter) dried tangerine peel (described on page 12)
- ¼ cup cold water
- 8 cups regular-strength chicken broth
- 1 large squab, Cornish game hen, or whole chicken breast
- 2 stalks celery with leaves removed
- 2 whole green onions
- 3 medium-sized Chinese fuzzy melon, peeled and halved (described on page 15)
- Chopped green onions for garnish

Soften tangerine peel in the water about 20 minutes; combine peel and water with the chicken broth, poultry, celery, onions, and melon in a 3 or 4-quart pan.

Bring to a boil, cover, and simmer about 45 minutes, or until poultry and melon are tender. Strain broth, discarding bones, skin, celery, onions, and peel. Salt to taste.

Serve a piece of melon, some meat, and some broth in each dish. Garnish with the chopped onions. Makes 6 servings.

Mandarin Mushroom Soup With "Singing" Rice

At the table you pour the hot soup over hot crisp-fried rice, which then hisses, sizzles, and "sings" for your supper.

This fascinating phenomenon delights children and adults alike.

- 2 cans (about 13 oz. each) regular-strength chicken broth
- ⅓ pound lean pork, finely diced
- 1 garlic clove, crushed
- 1 tablespoon soy sauce
- ¼ cup each sliced fresh mushrooms, sliced water chestnuts, and frozen green peas
- 1 recipe "Singing" Rice (recipe on page 61)

Pour chicken broth into a 1½-quart saucepan; add pork, garlic, and soy sauce and simmer for 10 minutes. Remove garlic and add mushrooms, water chestnuts, and peas. Simmer 2 minutes more. Turn into a warm heatproof pitcher or bowl with a pouring lip; keep hot in a 250° oven.

Fry the rice as directed and turn half of it into a preheated 1½-quart serving bowl. Immediately carry the soup and the tureen of rice to the table and quickly pour soup over the hot rice. Serve remaining rice in a bowl as an accompaniment to the soup. Makes 4 to 6 servings.

Soup with Bean Cake

Traditionally, the soft bean cake called for here is simmered in rich stock with meat and vegetables for a nourishing soup.

Substitute the more readily available Japanese bean cake, *tofu*, if you like.

- 8 cups regular-strength chicken broth
- 1 tablespoon soy sauce
- Dash sugar
- ¼ pound lean fresh pork
- 2 dried mushrooms, softened in ¼ cup water (described on page 16), or 1 can (about 4 oz.) sliced mushrooms
- 1 tablespoon chopped green onion
- 1 piece (about 1 lb.) "water" bean cake (suey dow foo, described on page 14)
- Chopped green onions for garnish

Combine the broth, soy sauce, and sugar in a 3-quart pan. Cut the pork into thin strips, about ¼-inch thick and 2-inches long. Rinse and slice dried mushrooms into thin strips. Bring the broth to a boil and add the pork, mushrooms and their liquid, onion, and bean cake. Simmer the soup about 25 minutes, or until pork is tender. Garnish with green onions. Makes 6 to 8 servings.

Won Ton Soup

Even if you serve Fried Won Ton for appetizers, you could still serve this soup because they taste so different boiled and then put in broth.

3 dozen filled but uncooked won ton prepared according to recipe for Fried Won Ton on page 34
   Boiling water
4 to 5 cups regular-strength chicken broth, canned or freshly made
½ teaspoon sesame oil (optional)
2 teaspoons soy sauce
3 green onion tops, sliced thinly

Drop filled won ton into a large kettle of boiling water. To prevent their sticking together, cook only a small number at a time. After they rise to top of water, simmer 4 minutes. Turn into colander, pour warm water over them; drain.

Heat chicken broth and season with sesame oil and soy sauce; then drop in won ton along with sliced green onion. Heat piping hot to serve. Makes 6 servings.

Dumpling Soup

This is a complicated dish for special occasions, but you can make the stock and two kinds of dumplings ahead—even freeze them. *See photograph on the opposite page.*

2 large cans (about 48 oz. each) regular-strength chicken broth (3 quarts)
1 large onion, sliced
¼ cup packed Chinese parsley (described on page 11), or 1 teaspoon whole coriander seed, crushed
2 slices fresh ginger root, or 1 teaspoon ground ginger
1 or 2 pounds bony chicken parts
1 recipe of Shrimp Dumplings (recipe on page 35)
1 recipe of Pork Dumplings (recipe on page 35)

Combine in a big, deep pan the chicken broth, onion, parsley or coriander, ginger, and chicken. Simmer, covered, for 1½ to 2 hours. Pour soup through a fine wire strainer, discarding residue. Return liquid to the large pan and heat to boiling; reduce to simmer and add dumplings.

Quickly return to simmer, then remove from heat and serve, spooning soup and dumplings gently into bowls.

You can make just half this recipe if you want to serve only one kind of dumplings in the soup. You can also refrigerate the soup, without dumplings, for several days, covered; or freeze until you are ready to heat and add dumplings. Makes 8 to 10 servings.

Winter Melon Soup

Winter melon soup is reserved for special occasions and is usually the first part of a multi-course dinner. This recipe contains more chicken to make a main-dish soup.

Because the soup steams inside the whole melon, you'll need a large kettle with a rack in the bottom (a canning kettle works well). For a 10-pound melon use a kettle 12 inches tall and 10 inches wide. In addition, you need a bowl that fits the melon base—to hold it upright during the cooking and serving. You can rig up a harness to lower and raise the melon in the kettle by knotting four lengths of heavy twine under the bowl.
The soup is pictured on the opposite page.

1 large stewing chicken, cut up
1 fresh pork hock
2½ quarts water
1 whole chicken breast
1 well-shaped (about 10 lbs.) winter melon (described on page 15)
6 dried mushrooms (described on page 16)
½ cup dried lotus seeds, optional (described on page 16)
1 piece, about 1½ inches in diameter, dried tangerine peel (described on page 12)
1 ounce Virginia ham or Italian prosciutto
2 dried duck gizzards, optional (described on page 12)
2 slices fresh ginger root
½ cup sliced water chestnuts
½ cup sliced bamboo shoots, optional
1 tablespoon sherry
1 teaspoon sugar
   Salt and pepper to taste

Cover the stewing chicken and pork hock with the water; bring to a boil, reduce heat, and simmer about 45 minutes. Add the whole chicken breast and simmer 15 minutes longer. Cut the breast from the stewing chicken and remove it and the other breast from the soup; set aside.

Continue cooking the remaining chicken and pork hock for several hours, or until a rich broth forms; strain, discarding chicken and pork.

Cut top off melon and reserve; scoop out seeds and stringy portions. Soak the mushrooms, lotus

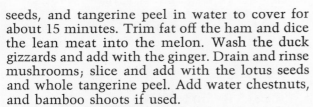

WINTER MELON SOUP (recipe on opposite page) is prepared in and served from the large melon.

DUMPLING SOUP (recipe on page 40) contains pork and shrimp dumplings, but can be made with one kind.

seeds, and tangerine peel in water to cover for about 15 minutes. Trim fat off the ham and dice the lean meat into the melon. Wash the duck gizzards and add with the ginger. Drain and rinse mushrooms; slice and add with the lotus seeds and whole tangerine peel. Add water chestnuts, and bamboo shoots if used.

Skim fat off chicken broth, reheat it, and season with sherry, sugar, and salt and pepper to taste. Set melon in a bowl, arrange twine harness, and lower into the cooking pan (with a rack in the bottom). Pour broth inside melon to fill it ¾ full; reserve any extra broth. Put top on melon, add water to outer pan to come about 2 inches up on the bottom of the bowl. Cover pan and steam over low heat about 3 or 4 hours. Cut the chicken breasts into about ½-inch cubes and add to soup just before removing from heat.

Lift melon, still sitting on bowl, out of the kettle; remove duck gizzards, tangerine peel, and ginger. Spoon some of the soft flesh inside the melon into each bowl when you serve. Refill melon with any extra chicken broth (heated). Makes 6 generous main-dish servings.

"One-Piece" Noodle Soup

In San Francisco's Chinatown many years ago this simple but authentic dish was a favorite, principally because it closely resembles chicken noodle soup. The name "one-piece" may indicate that noodles coiled in one clump were used (see photograph on page 10).

1 **pound thin, round noodles (described on page 9)**
  Boiling water
4 **cups regular-strength chicken broth**
1 **tablespoon soy sauce**
½ **teaspoon sugar**
1 **whole chicken breast, cooked, skinned, boned, and sliced in thin strips**

Cook noodles in boiling unsalted water until tender. Rinse in cold water and drain. Mound noodles in a deep serving bowl.

Bring to a boil the broth flavored with soy sauce and sugar. Pour over noodles. Garnish with chicken strips. Makes 6 to 8 servings.

MEAT MAIN DISHES, SOME WITH VEGETABLES

Although the Chinese do have some all-vegetable dishes, usually one or more vegetables are combined with small amounts of meat.

Mongolian Lamb With Spring Onions

Lamb is popular in the northern parts of China.

    1 pound boneless, fat-trimmed lamb (shoulder, leg, or loin), sliced ⅛-inch thick and cut in strips
    ½ teaspoon "five-spice" (description on page 11)
    1 egg white
    2 cloves garlic, slivered
    4 thin slices fresh ginger root
    3 teaspoons cornstarch
    5 teaspoons soy sauce
    6 tablespoons sherry
    2 tablespoons water
   10 green onions, including tops
    2 tablespoons salad oil

Mix lamb in a bowl with five-spice, egg white, garlic, ginger root, 1 teaspoon of the cornstarch, 1 teaspoon of the soy sauce; let stand 10 minutes. Meanwhile, blend rest of cornstarch, soy sauce, sherry, and water.

Cut white part of each onion in half, crosswise. Cut sections from green tops, about 1½ inches long.

Heat oil in a wide frying pan or wok over highest heat. Add meat mixture and cook, stirring, until meat browns slightly; return to bowl.

Add to pan the cornstarch-soy sauce mixture and white part of onion. Cook, stirring, until mixture thickens. Add meat and green tops and heat, stirring, until simmering. Serve at once.

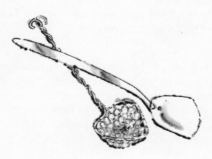

Tomato with Beef

You can season this dish with fresh ginger root or curry powder. It is good served over Fried Noodles, recipe on page 62.

    ½ pound beef round or flank steak
    3 medium-sized firm tomatoes
    1 or 2 small yellow onions
    1 small green pepper
    2 teaspoons cornstarch
    ½ teaspoon salt
    1 tablespoon soy sauce
    ¼ cup water
       Salad oil
    1 slice fresh ginger root, or ½ teaspoon curry powder
       Chopped green onions

Cut beef across the grain into strips about ⅛-inch thick and ½ by 2 inches. Cut tomatoes and onions in ½-inch wedges. Cut green pepper in uniform pieces about the same size as the wedges.

Combine cornstarch, salt, soy sauce, water, and 1 teaspoon oil; set aside.

Heat 3 tablespoons salad oil in a heavy frying pan or wok; add slice of ginger and the beef. Stir-fry until well browned, about 3 minutes. Add the onion, and curry powder if used; stir-fry a minute longer; add pepper, and fry several minutes.

Stir in the cornstarch mixture and stir 1 minute. Add tomatoes and cook 1 minute longer or until sauce is clear. Serve at once, garnished with green onions.

Greens with Beef

You can prepare this with a variety of greens.

  1½ pounds spinach, Swiss chard, celery cabbage, chard cabbage, or mustard cabbage (descriptions on page 15)
    2 tablespoons salad oil
    ½ pound flank steak or top round steak, cut 1-inch thick, then cut in strips ⅛-inch thick
       Sesame oil (optional)
    ½ teaspoon salt
    2 teaspoons soy sauce
    1 cup regular-strength chicken broth
    1 tablespoon cornstarch blended with ¼ cup water

Separate greens. (If using mustard greens, peel stalks.) Cut greens in 2½-inch-wide pieces. If stalks are thick, slash crosswise in 4 sections, cutting to within ½ inch of end of stalk. Let stand in cold water until ready to use; then drain well.

Heat oil over high heat in a wide frying pan or wok; add beef strips and toss and cook until meat is browned. Add 2 or 3 drops sesame oil, if desired, and sprinkle with half the salt and soy sauce; stir, remove meat.

Add enough additional oil to make 2 tablespoons in pan; add well-drained greens, stir and cook for about 3 minutes, or until greens are tender-crisp. Season with the remainder of the salt and soy sauce. Add broth.

Stir cornstarch and water; pour into pan, add meat, and cook until slightly thickened. Serve at once.

Green Beans with Beef

No special ingredient is needed for this simple recipe, but you can use Chinese "yard-long" beans if available.

½ pound fresh green beans or "yard-long" beans (described on page 14)
   Boiling water
½ pound beef top round or flank steak
2 teaspoons cornstarch
½ teaspoon sugar
1 tablespoon soy sauce
1 teaspoon salad oil
1 or 2 thin slices fresh ginger root
3 tablespoons salad oil
   Chopped green onion tops

Slice beans diagonally into 1-inch pieces. Drop into boiling water and cook until tender-crisp, 1 to 3 minutes. Drain, saving ⅓ cup of the liquid.

Cut beef into thin strips (about ⅛ by 1½ by ½ inches), slicing diagonally. Combine cornstarch, sugar, and soy sauce; add the 1 teaspoon oil and ginger root. Toss the beef in this sauce until well coated.

Heat the 3 tablespoons oil in a large frying pan or wok. Add the beans and stir-fry for 3 to 5 minutes over very high heat; remove from pan.

Remove the meat from the marinade; add beef to hot oil in frying pan, and stir-fry until browned, about 3 minutes. Return beans to pan along with the marinade and ⅓ cup of the bean-cooking water. Cook, stirring, until sauce is thickened and clear. Serve at once garnished with the chopped green onion tops.

Oyster Beef Slices

Personal preference accounts for the wide variety of oils used in stir-fry cookery. One Chinese woman makes a point of using lard for this dish.

1 pound beef steak (fillet or other tender fat-trimmed steak)
2 green onions with tops, thinly sliced crosswise
2 tablespoons each soy sauce and water
1 tablespoon each cornstarch and white wine (or water)
½ teaspoon salt
2 tablespoons lard or salad oil
2 tablespoons oyster sauce (description on page 11)
1 teaspoon sugar

Slice steak into strips ⅛-inch thick and about 1 by 2 inches.

Combine onions, soy sauce, water, cornstarch, wine, and salt. Pour over meat slices, and toss to coat meat.

Heat lard in large frying pan or wok until very hot. Turn in seasoned meat mixture; stir-toss over high heat for 2 minutes.

Add oyster sauce and sugar. Cook and stir just 1 minute more.

ESTIMATING SERVINGS FOR CHINESE MAIN DISHES

Because you may choose to serve only one, several, or many main dishes for a Chinese meal, it is impossible to state the number of people who can be served by each recipe. For this reason, most of the main-dish recipes here will not give you the number of servings each recipe makes (as *Sunset* recipes always do).

To estimate how many people the main dishes you have selected will serve, use this guide: Add up the *total number of pounds* of boneless meat, poultry, and seafood in all the main dishes you plan to cook. Then allow a total of ¼ to ⅓ pound of meat, poultry, and seafood per person.

In other words, if the total weight for all the dishes is 1 pound, they will serve 3 or 4 people. If the total is 2 pounds, they will serve 6 to 8 people. If the total is 3 pounds, they will serve 9 to 12 people.

Asparagus with Beef

The preparation of this dish in a Chinese pan (wok) is shown in *step-by-step photographs on the opposite page.*

These pictures also illustrate the wok cooking technique called stir-frying used for so many dishes and described in detail on page 17.

> 1 pound flank steak
> Salt
> 1 teaspoon cornstarch
> Soy sauce
> 2 pounds fresh asparagus with tight tips
> 2 medium-sized onions
> 2 cloves garlic
> Salad oil
> 3 tablespoons canned bean sauce (described on page 11)
> ½ teaspoon sugar

Cut steak lengthwise in 2½-inch strips, trimming off fat as you go. Then cut across the grain, in ⅛-inch-thick strips.

Put meat in bowl and add 1 teaspoon salt, cornstarch, and 2 teaspoons soy sauce. Wash asparagus carefully, break off tough ends, and cut diagonally into pieces about ¼-inch thick. (If you cut on a *sharp* diagonal, the pieces will be about 1½ to 2-inches long.)

Cut onions in half lengthwise, lay cut side down, and slice crosswise into ¼-inch slices.

Smash garlic cloves with flat side of knife or cleaver and remove skin.

Heat a wide frying pan or wok over *highest* heat, add ¼ cup oil; it should bubble slightly from the heat. Add garlic and cook just until pale brown. Remove and discard. Add meat, stir frequently, and cook until almost browned. Remove to a bowl.

Add 3 tablespoons more oil. Add onion. Cook a minute or two, stirring constantly. Make a little hollow on top of onion; add bean sauce. Cook until onion starts to get translucent. Add asparagus and sprinkle over 1 teaspoon salt, sugar, and 1 tablespoon soy sauce. Cover and cook, taking the top off occasionally to stir well, just until asparagus is tender-crisp.

Then, put the meat on top. Cook, stirring, just long enough to get the meat reheated. Serve at once.

Sweet & Sour Pork

You also can use this Sweet-and-Sour Sauce for crisp Fried Won Ton, recipe on page 34.

> Sweet-and-Sour Sauce (recipe follows)
> Marinade (recipe follows)
> 3 pounds lean pork butt, cut in 1-inch cubes
> About 1 cup cold water
> 6 tablespoons cornstarch
> Salad oil for deep frying
> 1 medium-sized onion, cut in 1-inch chunks
> 1 cup sliced celery (sliced diagonally about ¼-inch thick)
> 2 thin carrots, diagonally sliced ⅛-inch thick
> 1-inch piece fresh ginger root, peeled and cut in thin slivers (optional)
> 1 thin cucumber, sliced ⅛-inch thick
> 1 green pepper, seeded and cut in 1-inch squares
> 1 can (about 5 oz.) bamboo shoots, drained (sliced if not already)
> 2 tablespoons sesame seed, lightly toasted in dry frying pan
> A few Chinese parsley leaves, optional (description on page 11)

Prepare Sweet-and-Sour Sauce and Marinade.

Place pork in pan with the cold water. Cover, bring to boil, and simmer until tender, about 15 minutes. Drain. Pour Marinade over cooled pork, marinate 30 minutes (stirring occasionally), drain off. Dredge pork in the cornstarch.

Heat oil in a large frying pan or wok until very hot (about 390°). Fry pork, a few cubes at a time, until crisp and brown. Remove and drain on paper towels. Keep warm.

Pour off all but 3 or 4 tablespoons oil from pan and reheat until very hot. Toss in onion, celery, carrots, and ginger; stir-fry vigorously 1 minute. Add cucumber and pepper, fry 1 minute more. Add bamboo shoots, fry 1 more minute. Don't overcook.

Return meat to pan and pour in warm Sweet-and-Sour Sauce; stir until thoroughly hot. Serve at once, garnished with sesame and parsley.

Sweet-and-Sour Sauce. Mix ½ cup brown sugar, 2 tablespoons cornstarch, ½ cup cider vinegar, 1½ cups pineapple juice, and 2 tablespoons soy sauce in a saucepan. Cook over medium heat, stirring, until sauce thickens and becomes clear.

Marinade. Combine ½ cup soy sauce, 2 tablespoons sherry, 4 teaspoons sugar, ¼ teaspoon salt, 3 cloves garlic (minced or mashed), and a crushed 1-inch piece of fresh ginger root.

THE STIR-FRY TECHNIQUE SHOWN STEP BY STEP

FIRST STEP in stir-frying *Asparagus with Beef (recipe on opposite page)* is to cook the meat in a wok.

SECOND STEP, *after removing meat from pan, is to stir-fry onion; then add special Chinese bean sauce.*

NEXT, *ASPARAGUS is added to onion with seasonings and fried. Then pan is covered for brief steaming.*

LAST STEP: *return meat to wok and stir-fry dish just until hot, adding lid briefly to contain heat.*

PORK-STUFFED MUSHROOMS can be lowered into pan for steaming with this simple string harness.

Pork-Stuffed Mushrooms

Serve these as a main dish or appetizer. You can buy all ingredients at your supermarket. *Mushrooms are photographed above.*

  8 to 10 fresh mushrooms, each about 2 inches
       in diameter
½ pound lean pork (loin or well-trimmed butt),
       cut in small chunks
½ pound raw shrimp, shelled and deveined
  4 water chestnuts, finely chopped
  2 tablespoons cornstarch
½ teaspoon salt
  1 teaspoon sugar
  2 tablespoons soy sauce
  8 to 10 sprigs Chinese parsley, optional
       (described on page 11)

Wash mushrooms, dry, and remove stems without breaking cap (save stems for other uses).

Put pork and shrimp through the fine blade of a food chopper. Mix with water chestnuts, cornstarch, salt, sugar, and soy sauce, blending thoroughly. Divide meat mixture evenly among mushrooms, mounding into the cupped side.

Place filled mushrooms side by side in a 9 to 10-inch-diameter heatproof serving dish with a rim. Lay parsley over mushrooms.

Cover dish completely with a double thickness of waxed paper. Support dish on stand above 1 or 2 inches of boiling water. Cover pan snugly and simmer rapidly for 40 minutes. See information about steamers to buy or improvise on page 19 and a picture of a string harness to lift the dish out of the steamer in photograph above.

Turn off heat and remove lid, allowing steam to disperse; discard waxed paper. (If you like, discard the cooked parsley and garnish dish with a few fresh sprigs.) Lift dish from pan, dry base with a towel, and serve.

Pork Chow Mein

Chow means cooked by the stir-fry method. *Mein* means noodles, so serve either soft-fried or crisp-fried noodles with this. A recipe for both kinds is on page 62.

  1 cup regular-strength chicken broth, or 1 chicken
       bouillon cube dissolved in 1 cup water
  2 teaspoons soy sauce
      Salt to taste
  2 tablespoons cornstarch
½ pound pork shoulder
  4 to 6 stalks celery
  2 medium-sized onions
  1 can (about 1 lb.) bamboo shoots, drained
  1 can (about 4 oz.) sliced mushrooms, drained
      Salad oil

Put cold broth in a bowl and add soy sauce; season with salt until fairly salty. Stir in cornstarch until dissolved.

Slice pork in pieces ⅛ by ¼ by 1½ inches. Slice celery diagonally ⅛-inch thick. Slice onions in very thin slices or slivers. Cut bamboo shoots in ⅛ by ¼ by 1-inch sticks. (Mushrooms are already sliced.)

To a large frying pan or wok over highest heat, add 2 tablespoons oil. When hot, add pork strips; cook and stir 1 minute or until meat is browned but not dry. Remove meat.

Add 2 tablespoons more oil. When hot, toss in celery and onions; stir-fry 1 minute. Add bamboo shoots and mushrooms. Stir broth mixture and pour in. Stir and cook just until sauce is thickened. Add meat and stir until hot and sauce is clear. Serve immediately over noodles.

Black-Bean Spareribs

Probably these spareribs would be delicious even without the special black beans.

- **2 pounds spareribs, cut in 1-inch pieces**
  Boiling water
- **3 tablespoons fermented black beans**
  (description on page 11)
- **2 large cloves garlic**
- **2 thin slices fresh ginger root, minced, or**
  ⅛ teaspoon ground ginger
- **1 teaspoon each sugar, soy sauce, and cornstarch**
- **3 tablespoons each vinegar, chicken broth,**
  and dry sherry
- **2 tablespoons salad oil**
- **2 green onions, thinly sliced**

Drop the spareribs into boiling water, heat for 4 minutes, then drain and rinse in cold water (this removes excess fat).

Wash and drain the black beans and crush together with the garlic and ginger root. Combine the sugar, soy sauce, cornstarch, vinegar, chicken broth, and sherry.

Heat the oil in a large, heavy frying pan or wok. When hot, add spareribs and brown them quickly. Add black bean mixture and stir-fry a few seconds. Pour the soy sauce mixture over the spareribs. Add the onions. Cover and simmer, stirring occasionally, until tender, 35 to 40 minutes. (If necessary, add water, a little at a time, as the spareribs cook.)

Slivered Pork with Sausage

This recipe lets you sample the spicy-sweet Chinese sausages and easily experiment with the technique of steaming food.

- **6 dried mushrooms, each about 2 to 3 inches in**
  diameter (description on page 16)
  Hot water
- **1 pound boned, lean pork (butt or loin)**
- **5 teaspoons soy sauce**
- **3 tablespoons cornstarch**
- **¼ teaspoon sesame oil**
- **3 to 4 Chinese pork sausages (description on**
  page 12)

Cover mushrooms with hot water and let soak 1 hour; wash well. Squeeze mushrooms dry and slice in ¼-inch-wide strips, discarding stems.

Slice the pork across the grain into small bite-sized pieces ¼-inch thick.

Stir soy sauce, cornstarch, and sesame oil until blended (mixture will be very stiff), then stir in pork and mushrooms to mix well. Spread mixture evenly in a rimmed, heatproof serving dish about 10 or 11 inches in diameter.

Thinly slice sausages diagonally and arrange over pork. Cover top completely with a double thickness of waxed paper. Support dish on stand above 1 or 2 inches boiling water. See section on steamers to buy or improvise on page 19.

Cover pan snugly and simmer rapidly for 30 minutes. Turn off heat and remove lid, allowing steam to disperse; discard waxed paper. Lift dish from pan, dry base with a towel, and serve.

Fried Bean Cake
Stuffed with Pork

You can prepare this dish for steaming several hours ahead and refrigerate. Let warm to room temperature before cooking.

- **1 pound lean ground fresh pork**
- **4 water chestnuts, chopped**
- **2 green onions, chopped**
  Soy sauce
- **1 egg, slightly beaten**
  About 4 dozen fried bean cakes (dow foo pok,
  described on page 14)
- **1 can (14 oz.) regular-strength chicken broth**
- **1 teaspoon each cornstarch and water**

Mix together the pork, water chestnuts, onions, 1 tablespoon soy sauce, and egg. Carefully make a small slit in each fried bean cake and stuff with 1 teaspoon pork.

Place cakes in a shallow heatproof serving dish. Cover and put on a rack in a larger pan with 1 inch boiling water in it. See information about steamers to buy or improvise and how to use them on page 19.

Cover the large pan, and steam about 20 minutes.

To make gravy, heat together the broth and 2 teaspoons soy sauce. Mix the cornstarch and water, and stir into the broth; cook, stirring, until slightly thickened. Pour over the steamed cakes.

POULTRY MAIN DISHES, SOME WITH VEGETABLES

Chicken and duck are favored throughout China, prepared an infinite number of ways.

Cashew Chicken

Chinese dishes of this type are not cooked at the table, but this particular one adapts well to being prepared there, in an electric frying pan.

  3 whole chicken breasts
  ½ pound edible-pod peas or 2 packages frozen pods, partially thawed (description on page 14)
  ½ pound mushrooms
  4 green onions
  1 can (15 oz.) bamboo shoots, drained
  1 tablespoon chicken stock base dissolved in 1 cup water, or 1 cup regular-strength chicken broth
  ¼ cup soy sauce
  2 tablespoons cornstarch
  ½ teaspoon each sugar and salt
  ¼ cup salad oil
  1 package (4 oz.) cashew nuts

Bone chicken breasts and remove skin. Slice horizontally in ⅛-inch-thick slices, then cut in 1-inch squares. Arrange on a tray. Remove the ends and strings from fresh peas. Wash and slice mushrooms. Cut the green part of the onions into 1-inch lengths and then slash both ends several times making small fans; slice the white part ¼-inch thick. Slice bamboo shoots.

Arrange all the vegetables on the tray.

Pour chicken broth into small pitcher. Mix together soy sauce, cornstarch, sugar, and salt; pour into a small pitcher. Place oil and nuts in containers. Arrange at the table with electric frying pan.

To cook, heat 1 tablespoon of the oil over moderate heat (350°), add nuts all at once, and cook 1 minute, shaking pan, until lightly toasted; remove from pan and set aside. Add remaining oil to pan, add chicken, and cook quickly, turning, until it turns opaque. Add peas and mushrooms; pour in broth, cover, and simmer 2 minutes.

Add bamboo shoots. Stir the soy sauce mixture into the pan juices, and cook until sauce is thickened, stirring constantly; then simmer 1 minute uncovered. Mix in the green onions. Sprinkle with nuts.

Fresh Bean Cake With Chicken or Pork

This dish offers interesting texture contrasts.

  4 to 6 fresh bean cakes (dow foo, described on page 14)
  1 whole chicken breast, boned, or ¾ pound boneless lean pork
  2 dried mushrooms (described on page 16), soaked in water 30 minutes
  2 teaspoons bean sauce (described on page 11)
  1 teaspoon soy sauce
  ⅛ teaspoon sugar
  ½ teaspoon cornstarch
  ½ cup regular-strength chicken broth
  2 teaspoons salad oil
  1 can (5 oz.) sliced bamboo shoots, drained
     Chopped green onions for garnish

Cut the bean cakes into ½ by 1 by 1-inch blocks and set aside. Cut the chicken or pork into similar-sized pieces (you should have about 1½ cups). Rinse mushrooms and slice in thin strips, discarding stems. Mix bean sauce, soy sauce, sugar, cornstarch, and broth.

In a large frying pan or wok over high heat, sauté the meat in the hot oil about 2 minutes, turning to brown evenly. Add mushrooms, bamboo shoots, and bean cakes. Pour sauce mixture in the pan; cook, stirring carefully, until liquid is slightly thickened and smooth. Serve hot, garnished with green onions.

Chicken in Paper

Little paper envelopes containing chicken and seasonings are prepared ahead and deep-fried just before serving.

Pictures showing you how to fold the envelope packets are on the next page.

  2 pounds chicken breasts
  ¼ cup each soy sauce, sherry, and salad or sesame oil
     Piece of fresh ginger root (about 1 by 1 inch), cut in 40 fine slivers
     Chinese parsley, optional (see page 11)
     Salad oil

Cut pieces of bond or parchment paper, or aluminum foil, in 6-inch squares; cut about 20.

Skin and bone chicken and cut into pieces

CHICKEN IN PAPER (recipe on opposite page) is made by folding chicken inside paper, starting this way.

LAST STEP is to fold chicken packet over to form a small envelope; tuck upper flap in to seal packet.

about 1 by 1 by ½ inch. Marinate chicken for 1 hour in a mixture of soy sauce, sherry, and oil.

Place square of paper flat with one corner point facing you. Place drained chicken piece in the center and top it with 2 ginger slivers and a leaf of parsley. Fold into envelope packet this way:

Fold up bottom corner near you (over the chicken) to within 1 inch of the opposite top corner. This will form a triangle. Then fold right point of triangle over to within 3 inches of the left point and crease paper lengthwise (this means you are folding the right third of the triangle over to the left). See first photograph showing this step above.

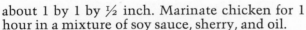

Then fold left point over to your right so that you fold over the left third of the triangle. Double the bottom part of the packet over toward the top point, as shown in the second photograph at the right above.

You now have a tiny envelope with a pointed flap sticking up as shown. Tuck this flap down inside the slot between the folded edges to secure the packet.

Just before dining, fry these little packages for 2 minutes in deep fat heated to 350°. Each guest opens his own, so large paper napkins or hot towels are in order. Makes 20 packets.

"Five-Spice" Chicken

Here you use ordinary spices to approximate the flavor of the Chinese "five-spice" described on page 11.

> 3 to 4 pound broiler-fryer chicken, cut into serving
>   pieces (preferably chopped into 1½-inch pieces
>   which can be picked up with chopsticks)
> ½ cup soy sauce
> ¼ cup chopped onion
> 1 clove garlic, crushed
> 1 teaspoon minced fresh ginger root
> ½ teaspoon cinnamon
> ¼ teaspoon each ground allspice and crushed
>   anise seed
> ⅛ teaspoon ground cloves
>   Dash black pepper

Marinate the chicken in the soy sauce, onion, garlic, and ginger root for 3 to 4 hours. Drain and arrange chicken in a shallow greased baking pan.

Mix spices, sprinkle over chicken, and bake in a 325° oven about 45 minutes to 1 hour, or until tender, turning once.

Lemon Chicken

This is a particularly delicious dish.

- 2 teaspoons each sugar and sesame oil
- ½ teaspoon salt
- ¼ cup cornstarch
- 3 tablespoons soy sauce
- 2 tablespoons sherry
- ¼ cup fermented black beans (see page 11)
- 1 clove garlic
  About 2½ pounds chicken thighs and legs, cut in 1 to 1½-inch lengths
- 1 lemon

Blend together smoothly the sugar, sesame oil, salt, cornstarch, soy sauce, and sherry. Rinse beans and drain well; mash with garlic, add to the cornstarch paste. Stir in the chicken pieces to mix thoroughly, then arrange pieces evenly in a 10 or 11-inch heatproof, rimmed dish.

Roll lemon to soften, then cut in half and squeeze juice over chicken. Cut the lemon shell into eighths and distribute over chicken. Cover top of dish completely with a double thickness of waxed paper. Support dish on stand above 1 or 2 inches of boiling water. See information on steamers to buy or improvise on page 19.

Cover pan snugly and simmer rapidly for 30 minutes. Turn off heat and remove pan lid, allowing steam to disperse. Lift dish from pan, dry base with a towel, and serve.

Jeweled Chicken

This sweet-sour dish is bejeweled with fruit.

- 3 whole chicken breasts (about 2½ lbs.)
- 1 egg white
  Cornstarch
- ¼ cup soy sauce
- 1 large can (about 1 lb. 4 oz.) litchis or longans (description on page 16)
- 2 tablespoons vinegar
- 2 tablespoons sugar
- ¼ cup salad oil
- 1½ tablespoons minced candied ginger (description on page 11)
  Parsley or Chinese parsley (see page 11)
  Sliced kumquats preserved in syrup

Remove skin and bones from chicken breasts. Thinly slice meat across the grain. In a bowl mix chicken thoroughly with egg white and 2 teaspoons cornstarch.

In another bowl gradually blend soy sauce with 1 tablespoon cornstarch; add 6 tablespoons of the canned litchi syrup, the vinegar, and sugar.

Heat salad oil over highest heat in a wide frying pan or wok. Add chicken mixture and stir constantly until the meat turns white. Then blend in minced ginger, drained litchis or longans, and the cornstarch-soy sauce mixture. Cook over highest heat, stirring, until sauce is thickened and clear. Serve garnished with parsley leaves and sliced kumquats.

Steamed Duck

This is an elegant dish for special occasions.

- 1 duck (about 5 lbs.)
- ⅓ cup soy sauce
  Water
- 4 to 6 dried mushrooms (described on page 16), or 1 can (3 to 4 oz.) sliced mushrooms
- 4 Chinese red dates (described on page 12), or ½ teaspoon brown sugar
- 2 pieces (each about 1½ inches in diameter) dried tangerine peel (described on page 12)
- ⅓ cup dry white wine
- 3 green onions
  Few pieces Chinese parsley (described on page 11), or a dash of ground coriander
- 2 cups hot water
- 4 stalks celery
- 2 tablespoons salad oil
- 1 small can (5 oz.) bamboo shoots, drained (sliced if not already)
- 2 tablespoons cornstarch
- ½ teaspoon sugar
  Lettuce leaves
  Chinese parsley and chopped green onions

Marinate the duck in soy sauce overnight or at least 6 hours, turning and basting occasionally.

About 20 minutes before you start cooking the duck, pour ½ cup cold water over the dried mushrooms (if you use them), dates, and tangerine peel in a bowl.

Drain the duck, pouring the soy sauce marinade into a large Dutch oven or deep frying pan, and bring to a boil. Put the duck in, breast down, and simmer very slowly about 3 minutes. Turn the duck on its back and simmer 3 more minutes, basting. Add the wine, and baste the duck with the wine and soy sauce mixture.

Remove 1 red date and 1 piece tangerine peel from the soaking water and put into the duck cavity, along with 1 green onion and pieces of parsley. Add the remaining red dates and tangerine peel to the liquid in the pan. Add the 2 cups hot water, cover, and simmer 2 to 2½ hours, or until the duck is very tender but not falling off the bones. Skim off the fat as the duck cooks, and baste with the liquid occasionally.

Slice the celery diagonally into ⅛-inch slices. Cut 2 remaining green onions into 1-inch lengths, then cut each piece into lengthwise slivers. If you are using the dried mushrooms, drain (saving the liquid), and cut them into ⅛-inch slices.

Just before serving, heat the salad oil in a frying pan, and stir-fry the bamboo shoots, celery, green onions, and mushrooms for 3 minutes. Add the liquid from the duck (about 1¼ cups) and simmer 5 minutes, uncovered. Combine the cornstarch, sugar, and 3 tablespoons of the liquid drained from the mushrooms; add to the vegetables, and cook, stirring, until the liquid is thickened, smooth, and clear.

Arrange the fresh lettuce leaves in a large, deep platter. Place the duck on top of the lettuce, and pour the vegetables and gravy over the duck. Garnish with parsley and chopped green onions.

Pot-Roast Duck

Taste-testers rated this an outstanding dish.

   4-pound duck
  ½ **cup soy sauce**
  1 **cup pearl barley**
     Hot water
  ½ **cup dried mushrooms (described on page 16)**
  3 **cups regular-strength chicken broth**
  4 **slices bacon, chopped**
  1 **medium-sized onion, chopped**
  1 **can (3 oz.) water chestnuts, drained and sliced**
  2 **tablespoons each sherry and soy sauce**
     Salt
  2 **tablespoons salad oil**
  1 **cup water**
     Cooked Cabbage (recipe follows)

Remove giblets and neck from duck and reserve; place duck in a large pan. Pour the ½ cup soy sauce over duck and let stand at room temperature for about 1½ hours, turning occasionally.

Cover barley with hot water and let stand 1 hour. Cover dried mushrooms with hot water and let stand 1 hour.

Drain barley and rinse well with cold water; drain again. Bring chicken broth to a boil, add

barley and duck neck, cover and simmer for about 30 minutes or until liquid is absorbed and barley is tender; stir occasionally. Discard duck neck. In a wide frying pan, cook bacon partially, add onion and sliced giblets, and continue cooking until onion is soft.

Rinse and drain mushrooms; chop, and mix with onions; add water chestnuts, sherry, and the 2 tablespoons soy sauce. Cook a few minutes more; add barley. Salt to taste.

Lift duck from soy sauce marinade. Fill breast and body cavity lightly with barley stuffing. Sew the cavities shut with heavy thread. Reserve any extra stuffing and reheat to serve with duck.

In a large heavy pan (deep enough to cover duck, heat the oil. Add duck and brown on all sides. Add 1 cup water, cover, and simmer slowly for 1½ hours or until duck is very tender.

Place duck on a bed of cooked cabbage on a serving dish. Skim fat from drippings. Cut duck with poultry shears or carve. Spoon some of the drippings over each serving of duck, stuffing, and cabbage.

Cooked Cabbage. Immerse 6 cups shredded white cabbage in 6 cups boiling, salted water. Drain cabbage as soon as water boils again. Season with 3 tablespoons melted butter, salt, and pepper.

Western-Style Peking Duck

True Peking Duck, named for the Chinese city, requires a day or more of preparation and some unique techniques. Chefs even disagree as to the exact method. Originally, only the skin of the duck was intended for consumption, but now everyone eats the meat, too.

Only a few hours are required for preparation of this version spiced and roasted in a simple manner to yield moist, succulent meat and tasty, crispy skin.

(Continued on next page)

PEKING DUCK (recipe begins on preceding page) is sliced off and placed in the middle of a round of Quick Thousand-Layer Bun. Condiments, in small dishes, are added; all is eaten like sandwich.

A menu featuring this duck is on page 26. *The dish is photographed above.*

2 **ducks, each 4½ to 5 pounds**
1 **teaspoon each ground ginger and ground cinnamon**
½ **teaspoon each ground nutmeg and ground white pepper**
¼ **teaspoon ground cloves**
2 **tablespoons soy sauce**
1 **tablespoon honey**
   Parsley or Chinese parsley for garnish (description on page 11)
8 **green onions, cut in thin slices (include some of the green tops)**
½ **to 1 cup canned Chinese plum sauce (description on page 12)**
   About ½ cup Chinese parsley (optional)
   Quick Thousand-Layer Buns (recipe on page 63)

Rinse ducks inside and out and pat dry; reserve giblets for other uses. Blend the ginger, cinnamon, nutmeg, pepper, and cloves. Dust ½ teaspoon of the spice mixture inside each duck, then rub the remaining spices evenly over the exterior of the birds. Close the abdominal cavity with small skewers. Wrap each duck separately in foil, folding the edges to seal tightly. You can do this ahead and chill.

Place ducks side by side in a large pan and bake in a 425° oven for 1 hour. Remove and let stand about 15 minutes, or until slightly cooled. Then carefully open foil at one end and drain out the accumulated juices and fat (the juices are good added to seasoned broth to make soup for another meal). Discard the foil.

Set ducks slightly apart on a rack in the baking pan and prick skin lightly all over with a fork. Bake at 375° for 30 minutes. Blend soy sauce with honey and brush onto ducks. Return ducks to oven and raise temperature to 500°. Bake about 5 minutes or until very richly browned; take care not to char.

Cut ducks in halves with kitchen scissors or poultry shears. Put a half on each serving plate and garnish with parsley. Set out the green onions, plum sauce, and chopped parsley in separate bowls or individual servings.

To eat, slice small pieces of skin and meat (trimming out fat) and put on a peeled-off round of a bun. Top with onion slices, a dab of plum sauce, and a few leaves of parsley, then fold bread around duck and eat with your hands.

SEAFOOD MAIN DISHES, SOME WITH VEGETABLES

Some of the most popular ways of cooking fish, shrimp, lobster, crab, scallops, and oysters are included in this section.

Seafood Cantonese

On a Chinese restaurant menu "Cantonese" or "with lobster sauce" indicates a sauce of fermented black beans, garlic, and egg. No lobster is in the sauce. It's just a sauce traditionally used for lobster, but good with other seafood.

The crab version features the crab still in the shell, a very messy but succulent dish to eat. Provide plenty of napkins and encourage finger-licking as necessary.

    1 pound medium-sized shrimp, or lobster tails,
        or 2 to 2½-pound Dungeness crab
    1 tablespoon fermented black beans
        (description on page 11)
    2 large cloves garlic
    2 tablespoons soy sauce
    ½ teaspoon sugar
    2 tablespoons salad oil
    2 ounces ground or finely chopped lean pork
        (optional)
    6 tablespoons boiling water
    2 teaspoons cornstarch
    1 tablespoon cold water
    2 tablespoons minced green pepper
    1 egg, slightly beaten

Shell and devein the shrimp; or wash the lobster tails and, if large, split through the shell lengthwise; or crack crab, clean and rinse well.

Wash and drain the black beans and crush with 1 clove of the garlic; mix in the soy sauce and sugar.

Heat the oil over high heat in a large heavy frying pan or wok. Add other clove of garlic and pork if used; brown quickly, then remove garlic. Add the seafood, the boiling water, and black bean mixture. Cover the pan and cook the prawns for 3 minutes or until pink (cook crab pieces for 3 minutes or lobster for 10 minutes).

Stir in a paste made by blending the cornstarch with the cold water; heat and stir until the sauce thickens and coats the shellfish. Add the green pepper and egg; heat and stir just until the egg sets. Serve immediately.

Cantonese Crab Curry

Curry powder is used in some Chinese dishes, particularly those from Canton.

    3 tablespoons salad oil
        About ½ cup finely chopped lean pork
    1 large clove garlic, minced or mashed
    1 teaspoon each salt and sugar
        About 4 teaspoons curry powder
    1 medium-sized onion, peeled and thinly sliced
    1 large green pepper, seeded and cut in
        ¾-inch squares
    2 large Dungeness crabs, cleaned, cracked, and
        with crab butter saved
    1¼ cups regular-strength chicken broth
    12 to 15 cherry tomatoes, cut in halves
    3 teaspoons cornstarch mixed with 2 tablespoons
        water
    1 egg, slightly beaten

Heat the oil in a large, heavy frying pan or wok. Add the pork and cook, stirring, over high heat until browned. Combine the garlic, salt, sugar, and curry; stir into the pork and oil.

Add the sliced onion and green pepper squares, and cook, stirring, for 2 minutes. Add the crab pieces, crab butter, and broth; cover and cook over high heat for 3 minutes. Add the tomatoes, then stir in the cornstarch-water paste.

Cook, stirring, for about 1 minute. Add the slightly beaten egg, and continue to stir just until the egg sets. Serve immediately.

Shrimp & Scallops With "Singing" Rice

At the table, you pour this hot dish over hot crisp-fried rice, which then "sings" and sizzles appetizingly.

- 1 cup sugar
- 3 tablespoons cornstarch
- 1 cup white rice vinegar (described on page 10), or ⅔ cup white vinegar with ⅓ cup chicken broth
- ¼ cup soy sauce
- 1 teaspoon grated fresh ginger root, or ¼ teaspoon ground ginger
- 2 cloves garlic, finely minced or mashed
- ¼ cup salad oil
- 1 pound each raw shrimp (shelled and deveined) and scallops (cut in halves)
- 2 green peppers, seeded and cut in 1-inch squares
- 2 red bell peppers, seeded and cut in 1-inch squares
- 2 thin carrots, thinly sliced
- 2 bunches green onions, cut in 1-inch pieces
- 1 can (8¼ oz.) bamboo shoots, cut in 1-inch squares
- 1 recipe "Singing" Rice (recipe on page 61)

Mix sugar, cornstarch, vinegar, soy sauce, ginger root, and garlic; set aside.

Heat salad oil in a 12-inch frying pan or wok over high heat. Add shrimp and scallops; stir and fry 3 minutes. Remove to a plate. Add to pan the green and red peppers, carrots, and white part of onions; stir and fry 2 minutes. Stir vinegar mixture and pour into frying pan with shrimp, scallops, onion tops, and bamboo shoots. Stir only until mixture thickens and sauce becomes clear. Turn at once into warm bowl, cover, and set into oven preheated to 250°.

Fry Singing Rice as directed, turn immediately onto a preheated serving platter, and bring to the table. Pour hot shrimp and scallops over hot rice.

Shrimp & Fl...

"Flower vegetable" is ... for cauliflower. Here fro... are used. They are two ... well and are handy for C...

- About 10 ounces raw shr... deveined
- ¼ cup salad oil
- 1 whole clove garlic, peeled
- 1 package (10 oz.) frozen caul...
- ⅔ cup water
- 1 teaspoon salt
- 1 package (10 oz.) frozen peas, un...ed
- 1 tablespoon cornstarch mixed with 2 tablespoons cold water

Cut shrimp into ½-inch lengths.

Heat oil in frying pan or wok over high heat; add garlic, and cook just until it becomes translucent (about 3 minutes); remove. Add shrimp and cook, stirring occasionally, just until color changes. Remove to a heated container; keep warm.

Place cauliflower in frying pan; cook 2 minutes, turning. Add the ⅔ cup water and salt. Cover and simmer 5 minutes. Add peas; cook 3 to 5 minutes after water returns to boiling (cauliflower should be slightly crisp).

Return shrimp to frying pan. Add cornstarch-water mixture; continue cooking gently and stirring until liquid thickens and becomes clear. Serve immediately.

Gingered Oysters

Those who enjoy oysters will find the seasonings in this simple dish delightful.

- 1 jar (10 oz.) small oysters, drained
- ⅛ teaspoon "five-spice" (description on page 11)
- 1½ teaspoons cornstarch
- 4 teaspoons soy sauce
- 3 tablespoons sherry
- 10 green onions
- 2 tablespoons salad oil
- 4 thin slices fresh ginger root

Mix oysters with five-spice, 1 teaspoon of the cornstarch, and 1 teaspoon of the soy sauce. Set aside for 5 to 10 minutes. Blend remaining cornstarch, soy sauce, and sherry; set aside.

Cut white part of each onion in half crosswise. Cut two sections from the green tops, each 1½ inches long; discard remainder.

Heat oil in a wide frying pan or wok over highest heat and add ginger root and white part of onions. Cook, stirring, about 30 seconds; remove onion from pan. Add oysters and spread out in pan. Cook over moderate heat, turning once, until oysters are firmed slightly—about 2 minutes.

Lift oysters from pan, let drippings brown, then blend in soy sauce-cornstarch mixture. Cook, stirring, until thickened, then blend in onions, green tops, and oysters, and heat until simmering.

Snow Peas with Shrimp

Snow peas are just one name for the edible pea pods used here. Frozen ones are available labelled "Chinese pea pods." If you find fresh ones, be sure to snap off the ends and string the pods as you would green beans.

14 large raw shrimp (20 to 30 count per pound)
½ teaspoon sugar
1 teaspoon soy sauce
1½ teaspoons cornstarch dissolved in 1 tablespoon water
3 tablespoons peanut oil
½ teaspoon salt
⅓ cup regular-strength chicken broth
½ cup thinly sliced water chestnuts
1½ cups edible-pod peas, or 1 package frozen pods, partially thawed (description on page 14)
½ large onion, cut in half crosswise then cut in small wedges
2 small stalks celery, cut crosswise in ¼-inch-thick slices

Shuck shrimp; cut in half lengthwise by cutting down through the rounded back side; lift out the sand vein. Mix the sugar, soy sauce, cornstarch, and water.

Heat oil in a large frying pan or wok over high heat; add the salt. Turn the shrimp all at once into the pan and stir and cook for 1 minute, or until shrimp turn white and pink. Add broth, water chestnuts, pea pods, onion, and celery. Cover and cook for 1½ minutes; remove cover once to stir.

Remove the cover and add the soy sauce mixture. Stir for 30 seconds, or until sauce is slightly thickened. Serve it at once.

Foo Yung

This favorite "omelet" can be made with crab, shrimp, or poultry.

You can even use slices of cooked meat, or make the dish completely meatless.

4 eggs, well beaten
1 package (about 8 oz.) fresh bean sprouts, or 1 can (1 lb.) bean sprouts, drained
⅓ cup thinly sliced green onions
1 cup (about 8 oz.) flaked, cooked crab meat or small shrimp, or slivers of cooked poultry
½ teaspoon salt
⅛ teaspoon pepper
⅛ teaspoon garlic powder
2 tablespoons salad oil
Foo Yung Sauce (recipe follows)

Combine eggs, bean sprouts, onions, seafood or poultry, salt, pepper, and garlic powder, mixing lightly. Omit the salt if using canned crab meat.

Heat the oil in a large frying pan, using just enough to coat pan; add remaining oil as needed. Using about ¼ cup of the mixture for each, fry patties as you would pancakes, turning once. Cook until set and lightly browned. Remove to a hot platter and pour the Foo Yung Sauce over.

Foo Yung Sauce. In a pan combine 1 teaspoon cornstarch, 1 teaspoon sugar, 2 teaspoons soy sauce, and 1 teaspoon vinegar; stir in ½ cup regular-strength chicken broth. Cook over low heat until thickened.

LINGCOD STEAKS (recipe at lower right) are moist and succulent because of steam-cooking method used.

Black-Bean-Steamed Fish

Use salmon, striped bass, halibut, or sea bass.

- 2 tablespoons fermented black beans (page 11)
- 1 large clove garlic
- 3 thin slices fresh ginger root, minced, or
  - ¼ teaspoon ground ginger
- ¼ cup soy sauce
- 1 teaspoon sugar
- 1 tablespoon salad oil
- 2 pounds fish steaks or fillets, ¾-inch thick
- 2 tablespoons sliced green onions with tops

Wash the black beans, drain, and crush to a paste with the garlic and ginger. Add soy sauce, sugar, and oil; mix thoroughly.

Arrange the fish in a single layer on a heat-proof plate (one that can be put into a steamer), or shape a plate of heavy foil. Spread top of fish evenly with the bean mixture. Arrange the plate on a rack or trivet over boiling water in a steamer. For information about steamers, see page 19.

Cover and steam for 10 minutes, or until fish flakes easily with a fork. Remove, sprinkle with the green onions, and serve immediately.

"Red-Cooked" Fish

Chinese call the gentle simmering of foods in soy sauce "red cooking," because the soy imparts a reddish color to the food.

- ¼ cup each water and chopped dried mushrooms (description on page 16)
- 2 pounds fillet of sole, or other mild white fish
- 1 tablespoon salad oil
- 2 thin slices fresh ginger root, minced
- 1 green onion, thinly sliced
- 2 tablespoons diced bamboo shoots
- ½ teaspoon salt
- ⅛ teaspoon crushed anise seed
- 2 to 3 tablespoons soy sauce
- 2 teaspoons dry sherry
- ½ cup regular-strength chicken broth

Wash the mushrooms well and soak in water about 5 minutes to soften before chopping (then soak in the ¼ cup water 20 minutes). Rinse the fish, dry, and lightly score the surfaces about 1½ inches apart. Heat the oil in a large frying pan and quickly brown both sides of the fillets. Remove from heat and sprinkle the mushrooms, ginger root, onion, bamboo shoots, salt, and anise seed over the fish.

Add the soy sauce, sherry, and chicken broth, bring the liquid quickly to a boil; then turn heat low, cover the pan, and simmer gently for 5 to 7 minutes, or until fish is tender and flaky.

Steamed Lingcod

A large supermarket specializing in foreign foods probably will carry the mushrooms and ginger. *The steamed fish is pictured on this page.*

- 6 to 8 dried mushrooms, 2 inches in diameter (description on page 16)
  Hot water
- 3 to 4 pounds lingcod, cut in steaks about 2-inches thick
- ½ teaspoon salt
- 2 slices fresh ginger root, each about ¼-inch thick, cut in slivers
- 1 tablespoon soy sauce

Cover mushrooms with hot water and let stand 1 hour; wash well. Pinch off and discard stems; squeeze mushrooms dry.

Arrange fish steaks close together in rimmed, heatproof serving dish about 10 or 11 inches in diameter; sprinkle with salt. Decorate the fish with ginger slivers and mushrooms. Cover dish completely with a double thickness of waxed paper and support above 1 or 2 inches of boiling water. For information about steamers to buy or improvise, see page 19.

Cover pan snugly and simmer rapidly for about 14 minutes, or until fish breaks easily when prodded lightly with fork in thickest part. To test, remove pan from heat, lift lid, and fold back a corner of the paper; be sure to cover fish and pan well for any additional cooking.

When done, remove from heat and take off pan lid to let steam disperse. Discard the waxed paper, lift out cooking dish, and dry the base with towel. Pour soy sauce over the fish steaks.

Smothered Rockfish

This recipe lets you sample several exotic seasonings, tangerine peel and red dates.

> 2 pieces (each about 1½ inches in diameter) dried tangerine peel (description on page 12)
> 1 Chinese red date (description on page 12)
> ¼ cup canned sliced mushrooms, drained; or 4 dried mushrooms (description on page 16)
> ⅓ cup cold water
> 3 pounds rockfish fillets (often called rock cod, sea bass, red snapper, Pacific Ocean perch)
> 2 tablespoons salad oil
> ¾ cup regular-strength chicken broth
> 1 tablespoon soy sauce
> ½ teaspoon each salt and sugar
> 5 thin slices peeled fresh ginger root, chopped
> ¼ cup each drained and sliced bamboo shoots and water chestnuts
> 1 tablespoon cornstarch dissolved in 1 tablespoon cold water

Soften the tangerine peel, date, and dried mushrooms (if you use them) in the ⅓ cup water for about 30 minutes. Rinse and drain. Thinly slice the mushrooms, discarding stems.

Brown the fish in the salad oil quickly on both sides, turning carefully. Add the chicken broth, soy sauce, salt, and sugar. Add sliced mushrooms, tangerine peel, date, ginger root, bamboo shoots, and water chestnuts.

Cover and cook over medium heat about 10 minutes, or until fish is flaky and tender. Add cornstarch-water mixture to the cooking liquid, cooking and stirring until thickened and clear. Pour vegetables and sauce over fish to serve.

DISHES WHICH SERVE AS A COMPLETE MEAL

The dishes in the following section are the easiest for a beginner at Chinese cooking because each one provides a full meal.

Chrysanthemum Bowl

Chinese recipes for dishes cooked at the table in a "hot pot" are numerous and varied. The most elaborate is the Chrysanthemum Bowl, a ceremony presided over by the hostess.

After all the foods are cooked and eaten, you sprinkle in a few chrysanthemum petals which contribute a spicy flavor to the broth. Then each guest poaches an egg in the broth, or beats the egg into it to make a soup.

See Cook-at-the-Table Equipment on page 19 for information about the "hot pot" (*photographed on the cover*) and substitute equipment. A menu featuring the dish is on page 30.

> Cooking Broth (see following recipe)
> Condiments, optional (suggestions follow)
> 1 or 2 whole chicken breasts, including the breast from the chicken used for the Cooking Broth
> 1 to 2 pounds spinach
> ½ head celery cabbage (description on page 15)
> 1 pound white firm-fleshed fish, such as halibut or swordfish
> 1 cup small oysters
> ½ pound raw, peeled, and deveined small shrimp
> ½ pound pork tenderloin
> ½ pound chicken livers or 2 pork kidneys (optional)
> ¼ pound thin translucent noodles (description on page 9)
> Salad oil
> 2 large white "pompon" chrysanthemum blossoms
> 6 raw eggs
> Hot steamed rice

Prepare Cooking Broth and Condiments.

Slice the chicken breast very thin. Remove tough stems from the spinach; stack each 5 or 6 leaves together, then cut in 3 or 4 diagonal slices. Slice the cabbage diagonally about 1½ inches wide. Slice fish. Leave oysters and shrimp whole. Slice pork very thin. Blanch the chicken livers or kidneys and slice thin.

You can do all the necessary cooking, cutting, and arranging of these foods in bowls or on trays several hours in advance; cover and refrigerate.

No more than 30 minutes before dinner, fry the translucent noodles, a few at a time, in salad oil heated to 390°; they will immediately puff and turn white (try out a few strands first, so that you will be prepared). Remove at once and drain.

Wash the blossoms well and lay on the table near where the cooking pot will be. Leave eggs in shells and put one at each guest's place.

Procedure for cooking at the table: Bring the cooking pot to the table containing about half of the hot broth (1 quart); surround it with containers of foods to be cooked. There are two different ways to approach the cooking, depending partly upon how adept your guests are with chopsticks.

The traditional way is to pass the dishes of food so each guest can take onto his plate some of each. Using chopsticks, each puts his own meat, vegetables, and noodles into the simmering broth; and, when done to his liking, removes them to his plate, then dips each morsel in the condiments.

Or, for a faster start to this meal, the hostess can put into the pot about half of each of the ingredients, keeping foods as separate from each other as possible, cover the pan, and let the ingredients cook about 5 minutes. Guests then serve themselves.

When all the foods have been cooked, add the flower petals to the rich stock remaining. Each guest can then either beat an egg in his soup bowl and ladle some of the hot broth over it; or—and this is a real trick—break his egg into the cooking pot, poach it, and remove it to his plate with chopsticks. (We suggest you have on hand a slotted spoon or "leaking ladle," the Chinese name for the wire ladle pictured on page 20.) Recipe serves 6 people.

Cooking Broth. You can prepare this the day before your dinner. Start with a large broiler-fryer or small roasting chicken (about 4 pounds); carefully remove the breast and reserve. Cut up the remaining chicken and put into a large pot with 2½ quarts water and ¼ cup soy sauce. Bring to a boil and simmer about 1 hour. Cool and strain the broth (use the cooked meat for a salad or casserole).

Or use canned chicken broth seasoned with the soy sauce if you want to save time.

Condiments. Serve soy sauce, Chinese oyster sauce, and minced green onion in small dishes. You may prefer to dilute the oyster sauce with some of the broth for a dipping sauce. Oyster sauce is described on page 11.

"Hot Pot"

In China and neighboring countries, rooms once were heated with charcoal in a small brazier. To conserve precious fuel, it was common to set a pot of broth over it and cook small pieces of food for a long, leisurely supper. Then a special cooking vessel called the "hot pot" was designed for this meal. See the section on page 19 called Cook-at-the-Table Equipment for details about this pot and information on substitute equipment you may already own.

A menu featuring this one-pot meal with serving suggestions is on page 27. *The pot is photographed on the cover and on page 28.*

Chicken broth (canned or homemade)
White rice or thin noodles (vermicelli, Chinese mein, or Japanese somen described on page 9)
A selection of meats, seafood, and vegetables (see suggestions following)
Sauces (see suggestions following)

To estimate the quantity of broth needed, first fill your cooking pot with water, about three-quarters full. Measure the water and also allow extra broth for adding as foods cook.

To estimate quantity of rice, allow ½ cup (uncooked) for 4 persons; allow ¼ pound uncooked noodles for 4.

Prepare your choice of meats, seafood, and vegetables. The traditional Chinese way of presenting the foods to be cooked is to arrange each kind attractively on its own plate. This means the guests have to pass plates periodically if the plates aren't within reach. If table space permits, you might set up two plates of each food so that a complete selection is on either side of the cooking pot.

Another way is to prepare a combination plate of uncooked meat, fish, poultry, and vegetables for each person. Have all foods cut as suggested.

Shortly before dinner, cook noodles or rice, cover, keep warm. (They will be added to broth at end of meal to make soup.)

Just before the meal starts, fill the cooking container about three-quarters full of boiling chicken broth. Cover and return the broth to boiling; then seat the guests. Have more broth ready to add as needed.

To cook dinner, each person puts about 3 items in an Oriental wire ladle (see sketch on page 20) and holds it in the broth until the foods are just cooked; most take 1 minute or less. (Or just put foods in broth and fish them out with chopsticks or slotted spoon when done.) Dip cooked foods in one of the sauces to eat.

When your guests have finished meat and vegetables, add warm, drained cooked noodles or rice to the rich broth, bring to boiling, then ladle soup into individual bowls.

Meats, Seafood, and Vegetables. Tender meats, fish, poultry, and vegetables are all suitable. In the list below, some of the foods are traditional to the Chinese hot pot, some are adaptations.

For four persons, select six to eight foods (four or five meats and two or three vegetables):

About ¾ pound flank steak; slice partially frozen meat very thin (cut steak in half lengthwise, then cut in ⅛-inch slices across the grain)
¾ pound boneless lean lamb, cut same as flank steak, above
1 whole boned chicken breast, cut in strips and marinated several hours in mixture of 2 tablespoons each soy sauce and salad oil, 1 teaspoon chopped fresh ginger root, and 1 clove garlic
1 pound medium-sized shrimp, shelled, sliced lengthwise, and deveined
¾ pound scallops, rinsed, dried, cut in half
1 jar (10 oz.) oysters, well drained
1 pound fresh soy bean cake (dow foo or tofu, description on page 14)
1 can (1 lb.) abalone, drained and sliced very thin
¼ medium-sized head celery cabbage separated into leaves (description on page 15)
½ bunch spinach, separated into leaves with stems cut off
¼ pound fresh mushrooms, sliced
¼ pound edible-pod peas (description on page 14)
1 small head cauliflower broken into bite-sized pieces
½ pound tender asparagus, cut in 1½-inch lengths
1 small bunch broccoli, cut in bite-sized pieces
2 medium-sized turnips, thinly sliced
Chopped green onion, parsley, or Chinese parsley for garnishing plates (description of parsley on page 11)

Sauces. Select several from the following list. Chinese sauces are described on page 11.

Hot Chinese mustard (mix dry mustard to a paste with water)
Soy sauce
Teriyaki sauce
Chinese oyster sauce
Chinese plum sauce
Chinese hoi sin sauce

MANDARIN PANCAKE dinner (recipe below) consists of thin pancakes wrapped around fillings and sauce.

Mandarin Pancake Dinner

The photograph above illustrates the pancakes and fillings for this simple one-dish meal. A menu and serving tips are on page 29.

Mandarin Pancakes (recipe on page 63)
Beef Filling with Hot Chile (recipe follows)
Chicken Filling with Bean Sprouts (recipe follows)
Egg Filling with Scallops (recipe follows)
Sauces (suggestions follow)

To eat, fill a steamed pancake sparingly with one of the three fillings, dab on a bit of sauce if you wish, roll up the pancake, and fold one end to hold in the juices. Eat out of hand. Serves 4.

Beef Filling with Hot Chile. Cut 1 pound fat-free, boneless beef sirloin in paper-thin strips. Combine with 3 tablespoons soy sauce, 1 tablespoon sherry, 2 teaspoons cornstarch, and ½ to 1 teaspoon liquid hot-pepper seasoning (add half now and the rest at serving time to suit your taste). Cover the meat and chill until ready to cook.

(Continued on next page)

Heat 3 tablespoons salad oil over highest heat in wide frying pan. Add meat mixture and cook, stirring constantly, until meat loses pink color. Put meat in serving dish, garnish with radish slices, and serve at once (or keep warm).

Chicken Filling with Bean Sprouts. Bone and remove skin from 1 large whole chicken breast (you need about ½ pound boneless meat). Thinly slice the breast and mix thoroughly with 1 egg white and 1 teaspoon cornstarch. Cover and chill.

Wash and drain 12 ounces fresh bean sprouts or a 1-pound can of sprouts. Combine in a bowl with 1¼ teaspoons salt and 1 teaspoon vinegar. Cover and chill until ready to cook.

Heat 3 tablespoons salad oil over highest heat in a wide frying pan. Add chicken and stir constantly until it turns white, then add bean sprout mixture and continue to cook until sprouts are hot. Serve at once (or keep warm several minutes until all dishes are prepared) garnished with parsley sprigs or chopped green onion.

Egg Filling with Scallops. Drop 1 cup or about ¾ pound scallops (cut large scallops in half) into enough boiling, salted water to cover and simmer for 3 minutes. Drain well and chill covered, until ready to use.

Beat 5 eggs to blend with ½ teaspoon salt; stir in scallops. Cook 3 tablespoons finely chopped leek or onion until soft in 3 tablespoons salad oil over medium heat in a wide frying pan. Pour in egg mixture and cook, stirring, until eggs are set. Garnish with leek slices or parsley sprigs and serve at once.

Sauces. You might like to offer at least one or two Chinese sauces such as plum, hoi sin, oyster, or hot mustard—described on pages 11 and 12.

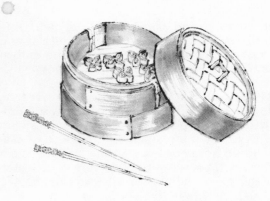

RICE, DUMPLINGS, NOODLES & BREADS

Not only do the Chinese eat rice and noodles, but they also eat pancakes and breads.

Chinese Rice

Chinese rice is quite firm and dry, but the grains stick together enough to manage with chopsticks. For a description of types of rice, see page 8.

> 1 cup long or medium-grain rice
> ½ teaspoon salt (optional)
> 1½ to 2 cups cold water

Put rice in a heavy pan which has a tight lid. Add salt if desired (Chinese wouldn't use it), and cold water. The exact measure isn't very important. The Chinese use the finger to judge the height of water about 1 inch above the rice—about the length to the first joint.

Set pan over high heat and boil rapidly, uncovered, until most of the water has been absorbed; stir often (with fork or chopstick) while it is boiling to prevent sticking.

Turn heat to lowest setting, put on lid, and allow the rice to steam undisturbed for 20 to 30 minutes, depending upon how soft you like rice. Makes 4 or 5 servings.

Fried Rice

This is a family, leftover dish in China. But Americans like it, so restaurants here serve it.

> 2 eggs, beaten
> 3 tablespoons salad oil
> 1 cup finely shredded or diced cooked shrimp, ham, pork, or beef (optional)
> 6 green onions including tops, thinly sliced or chopped
> 4 cups cold cooked rice
> 2 tablespoons soy sauce
> ½ teaspoon sugar
>   Salt if needed

Method 1: Fry beaten eggs until firm in the oil, remove from heat, and cut into shreds. Return egg to frying pan with meat (cut into shreds to match eggs). Add onion. Cook over medium heat, stirring constantly, for 3 or 4 minutes. Add the rice. Mix the soy sauce, sugar, and salt if needed; dribble over the rice. Stir until rice is hot. Serves 6.

Method 2: Sauté rice in oil over medium heat about 15 minutes, or until it is golden brown. Add meat if desired. Pour beaten eggs over rice. Cook, stirring often, until the egg is set. Sprinkle with the onion and soy sauce mixed with the sugar and salt if needed. Stir just until blended. Serves 6.

"Singing" Rice

Sometimes called "sizzling," this hot crisp rice also snaps, crackles, and pops when you pour hot food over it at the table.

Legend says a frantic hotel chef invented it from leftovers when an emperor arrived unexpectedly. The dramatic dish made such an impression that the chef was hired to cook at court.

Two recipes utilize this rice: Mandarin Mushroom Soup on page 39 and Shrimp and Scallops on page 54.

    1   cup long-grain (regular) rice
    4   cups water
    2   teaspoons salt
        Salad oil for deep frying

A day or more in advance, combine rice, water, and salt in a 2-quart saucepan. Let stand ½ hour. Bring to a boil, cover, and simmer 30 minutes. Drain.

Spread evenly on a heavily greased cooky sheet. Bake in a 250° oven for about 8 hours, opening the oven door occasionally and turning rice with a spatula. Break the crusty rice into bite-sized pieces. You can store in airtight containers or bags in your refrigerator for weeks.

Just before serving time, turn on oven to 250° and warm the serving platter or soup tureen; also heat a bowl or pitcher to bring the food which will be poured over the rice to the table.

Pour salad oil about 2 inches deep in a 6-quart saucepan or deep-fat fryer with a basket; heat to 425°. Fry rice (stirring with a slotted spoon) until it is golden brown, about 4 minutes. Drain briefly; transfer to warmed serving platter or soup bowl. Bring to the table, and immediately pour hot soup or entrée over the rice.

(Be sure rice, food, and containers are hot.)

NOODLES IN BROTH (recipe below) are easy to prepare. Many kinds of noodles can be served this way.

Noodles with Sauce

Several very simple boiled noodle dishes can take the place of rice at any meal. You can even cook the noodles ahead and reheat them as the instructions tell you.

Information about various types of noodles, how long to cook them, and Japanese or Italian substitutes for Chinese types is on page 9.

Cook ½ pound noodles (any kind except translucent ones) in unsalted water until barely tender. Rinse in cold water and drain.

To serve, reheat by dunking in hot water; drain. Toss noodles with ¼ cup soy sauce and 2 tablespoons salad oil or sesame oil. Sprinkle sparingly with cayenne. Makes 4 to 6 servings.

Or mix noodles with ¼ cup chopped green onion tops and ¼ cup Chinese oyster sauce described on page 11. Chinese shrimp-flavored noodles are particularly good this way.

You also can reheat noodles in a small amount of rich chicken or beef broth. Serve in bowls, preferably individual ones. Top with slices of cooked chicken, barbecued pork, or fried shrimp (*as shown in the photo above*).

Won Ton Noodles

Won ton noodles or "skins" are 3-inch squares of thin dough used for many dishes. They are usually filled with meat or seafood mixtures and folded various ways.

Then, they may be crisp-fried; a recipe for Fried Won Ton is on page 34. Or they may be simmered like dumplings in soup. A Chinese Won Ton Soup recipe is on page 40 and a Korean version, Dumpling Soup, on page 91.

2   **cups regular all-purpose flour**
3   **eggs**
1   **teaspoon salt**
    Cornstarch

Sift flour before measuring. Beat eggs very slightly with the salt. Mix into flour and knead until *very* smooth and elastic. This takes time unless you have a heavy-duty kitchen mixer. Divide dough in fourths. Work with one piece of dough at a time and keep the others covered with clear plastic film. Sprinkle a rolling pin (preferably the long slim French type, without handles) with cornstarch and sprinkle a board with cornstarch. Roll the dough into a long rectangle as thin as possible. Sprinkle dough with cornstarch as you work. Let dough rest about 10 minutes, then continue rolling until about 1/16-inch thick or even thinner. Cut rectangle into 3-inch squares.

Each quarter of dough makes 1½ to 2 dozen 3-inch squares. Stack squares with cornstarch between and wrap in plastic film; proceed same way with remaining dough. Freeze if you like. Brush off cornstarch before using. Makes 6 to 8 dozen squares.

Fried Noodles

There are two ways to fry noodles, called soft-fried and crisp-fried. Soft-fried are sautéed in oil until slightly translucent and still moist. Crisp-fried noodles are deep-fried in oil until medium-brown and very crunchy (like Chow Mein noodles you buy in cans, but better because they are fresher and hot).

In either case you must boil dry, packaged noodles, drain, rinse in cold water, drain again, separate, pat as dry as possible with paper towels, and dry in the air 30 minutes before cooking so the oil does not splatter. For information about types of noodles and how long to boil them, see page 9.

Fresh thin noodles may be crisp-fried without being cooked if they are soft and moist.

You can serve fried noodles on the side or underneath many Chinese dishes.

Soft-Fried Noodles. Either thin, round noodles or the wide, flat kind can be used. Boil noodles and prepare as described above. For each half pound of noodles before cooking, heat ¼ cup salad oil over highest heat in wok or large frying pan (well cured or with nonstick flurocarbon finish). Add a clump of noodles. Sauté, keeping the noodles in motion but not mashing them, until translucent, 3 to 5 minutes. Makes 4 to 6 servings.

Crisp-Fried Noodles. Thin, round noodles work best because they puff up to greater size. Boil noodles (if not fresh ones) and prepare as described above, drying thoroughly. Separate strands and cut long ones into shorter lengths. Heat several inches of salad oil to 365°. Drop in a small amount of noodles at a time, turning them in the oil to keep separate. Fry until golden or even a medium-brown. Remove with a slotted spoon and drain on paper towels. Keep warm.

Mandarin Pancakes

The various English names also include Chinese doily, Peking doily, and Chinese tortilla.

Just imagine a Mexican flour tortilla, thin as parchment, then made even thinner by being split after it is cooked. (It splits easily because you made it by putting together two uncooked rounds with oil between.) Just follow steps in recipe and in *photographs on the next page.*

You can make the pancakes as long as a day ahead if you wrap them airtight.

The pancakes are used for a special Mandarin pancake dinner. See dinner recipe on page 59 and menu on page 29.

2 cups unsifted all-purpose flour
¾ cup boiling water
About 2 tablespoons sesame oil or salad oil

Measure flour into a bowl and mix in the boiling water with a fork or chopsticks. Work dough several minutes until it holds together, then knead on a lightly floured board for 10 minutes or until very smooth and velvety. Cover and let stand for 30 minutes.

Roll dough into a 12-inch-long log. Cut in 12 equal pieces; cover with plastic wrap and keep each covered until you roll it out.

To make each pancake, cut a piece of the dough exactly in half. Shape each section into a ball and flatten slightly. Roll each ball on a very lightly floured board to a round 3 inches in diameter. Brush sesame oil lightly on top of one round and cover with another round. Press the two rounds lightly but firmly together to align them securely.

Place the double round on a lightly floured board and roll out with even, gentle pressure to 7 or 8 inches in diameter (perfect rounds are not a necessity). Turn frequently, brushing board lightly with flour as needed. Do not get wrinkles or folds in the cake.

Repeat procedure to make each pancake. Make only 2 or 3 at a time, then cook before making more. Keep uncooked pancakes tightly covered with clear plastic wrap.

Heat a wide frying pan over medium-high heat, then place a pancake on the ungreased surface. Turn about every 15 seconds until cake is blistered generously by air pockets, turns a slightly translucent, parchment color, and feels dry. The cake should not brown, but a few golden spots are not harmful. If overcooked, the cake becomes brittle.

Remove from pan and carefully pull the two halves apart, starting where you see the cakes join. Stack halves and keep tightly covered. Cook remaining cakes. Wrap airtight.

To heat for serving, line a flat-bottomed steamer with a towel dipped in water and wrung dry; stack the pancakes inside towel. See section on steamers on page 19.

Cover; place over simmering water for 10 minutes. Fold hot pancakes in triangles and arrange in serving basket. Since they dry out quickly, serve just a few at a time and keep the remainder in the steamer. Makes 24 pancakes.

Quick 1000-Layer Buns

Just as 1000-year-old eggs are not that old, these buns do not have that many layers (just 4 in this version).

The buns are used to eat Western-Style Peking Duck, recipe on page 51.

But they would also be good with barbecued pork that you can buy at Chinese markets or make by the recipe on page 33.

In either case, you peel off a layer of bun and wrap it around the meat to eat sandwich fashion. Spread with hot mustard if you like.

2 packages refrigerator biscuits (10 biscuits per package)
Salad oil or sesame oil

Cut each biscuit in half to make 40 pieces. Roll 30 pieces out individually on a well-floured board to make rounds about 2½ inches in diameter; they immediately shrink back to about 2 inches diameter, the size you want. Roll the remaining 10 pieces into rounds about 3 to 3½ inches in diameter.

Brush the tops of the small rounds with oil and stack in threes. Cover each stack with a large round, and gently pull dough down to cover stack, tucking under bottom side. Brush bun tops with salad oil and set each one separately on a small square of oiled foil. (You can cover buns and chill several hours.)

Arrange buns, each on its foil square, side by side, on a rack in a steamer. For information about steamers you can buy or improvise, see page 19.

Do not stack buns in steamer; cook in sequence if necessary. Cook, covered, over boiling water for 10 to 12 minutes, or until buns look rather translucent and no longer feel sticky and soft. Keep warm over hot water. Peel apart to eat. Makes 10.

FOUR STEPS IN MAKING MANDARIN PANCAKES

PANCAKE DOUGH (recipe on preceding page) is cut, rolled in rounds; two rounds are pressed together.

DOUBLE ROUND is rolled very thin and cooked like a pancake (flipped like flapjack if you know how).

COOKED PANCAKE is pulled apart into two thin pancakes; halves are heated in bamboo steamer.

STEAMED PANCAKES are folded in triangles and placed in napkin-lined basket so they will stay hot.

DESSERTS, SWEETS & BEVERAGES

There's no need to serve dessert with Chinese meals at all. But if you prefer one, there are several simple things to make or buy.

Desserts You Can Buy

The Chinese have few desserts and most of their sweets are served at tea time. However, there are some simple things you can buy if you want to serve dessert to Americans.

Fresh fruit is always appropriate. You can make a pyramid of whole oranges, tangerines, peaches, nectarines, pears, or apples (such fruit towers are seen as offerings in Buddhist temples and are typical "good luck" arrangements everywhere).

Persimmons or melon are good in season. The Chinese particularly relish watermelon. Many varieties, including yellow ones, are served in China.

A fruit compote also is typical, such as this one:

Litchi Compote. Peel 1 small pineapple, core and cut fruit in bite-sized pieces. Mix with 1 large can (1 lb. 4 oz.) litchis or longans, 1 can (about 15 oz.) peeled, seeded muscat grapes, and ⅔ cup *each* of the litchi and muscat syrups. Chill at least several hours. Garnish with mint leaves. Makes 6 servings. (Litchis and longans are described on page 16 of the Ingredient Shopping Guide chapter.)

For just a bit of sweetness, you can serve a piece of candied or preserved ginger or preserved kumquats (both available at supermarkets or you can preserve kumquats at home by the recipe on the next page).

Chinese candied coconut or melon, or dried litchi nuts in the shell (available at Chinese markets and sometimes in cellophane packages near the cash register in Chinese restaurants) make an interesting small sweet finale.

Fortune cookies and almond cookies may be sold in cellophane bags at your supermarket. Chinese sesame cookies may also be there, or at Chinese shops. Any sesame cooky would be good.

At Chinese bakeries you may find other kinds of cookies, coconut and custard tarts, and steamed sponge cake.

Ice cream flavored with ginger or litchi nuts is sold by some Chinese ice cream makers, who also provide it to restaurants.

Candied Vegetables

Chinese confectioners make a fine art of preserving fruits and vegetables by crystallizing them in a simple sugar syrup. Serve for dessert or with tea in the afternoon.

In the Chinatowns of large cities, you can find shops which sell a large variety of candied vegetables, including some more exotic types such as lotus root slices. Some shops provide pretty boxes to contain an assortment for a gift.

6 cups sugar
3 cups water
6 cups vegetables (see kinds and directions following)

Combine sugar and water in a wide, shallow saucepan. Bring to a boil and simmer 10 minutes. Add vegetables about 1 cup at a time or enough to make a single layer in bottom of the pan. Return to boil, then simmer gently for the length of time given below for each vegetable. You can cook all of the vegetables in the same syrup except beets (beets and carrots can cook in the same syrup).

Lift vegetables from syrup with a slotted spoon and arrange in a single layer on wire racks over a pan to catch the drip. Let stand overnight lightly covered with waxed paper (do not use foil). Cover and save syrup.

Next day reheat syrup to boiling, add vegetables in small quantities as before, and simmer for 2 minutes. Lift from syrup and return to wire racks; cover lightly with waxed paper and let stand overnight.

Repeat this cooking and draining process 3 or 4 more times (a total of 5 to 6) or until vegetables are firm and dry to the touch. Roll in granulated sugar and store airtight, or wrap airtight and freeze.

Vegetables. *Canned whole green beans:* drain thoroughly and cook in the syrup 3 minutes for the first step.

Canned sliced beets: drain and cook in the syrup 3 minutes for the first step.

Raw carrots: peel, slice diagonally about ⅜-inch thick and cook in the syrup 5 minutes for the first step.

Raw zucchini: cut off stem ends, slice diagonally about ½-inch thick and cook in the syrup 5 minutes for the first step.

Raw turnips or rutabagas: peel, slice about ⅜-inch thick (cut slices in halves or quarters) and cook in the syrup 5 minutes for the first step.

Almond Cookies

This recipe accurately duplicates Chinese almond cookies. Lard and slow baking are the secrets of success.

Substitute unblanched almonds or even peanuts if you like. Pine nuts, used in Northern Chinese cooking, also would be good.

    1   cup (½ lb.) lard
    1   cup sugar
    ¼   teaspoon almond extract
        Few drops yellow food coloring (optional)
    3   cups unsifted regular all-purpose flour
        About 36 whole blanched almonds
    1   egg yolk
    2   tablespoons water

Cream lard with sugar until fluffy, then blend in almond extract and enough food coloring to tint mixture a light yellow. Thoroughly mix in the flour 1 cup at a time; the last addition makes the mixture crumbly.

To shape each cooky, measure 1 level tablespoon of the dough and press with your hands to form a flat round cake about 1¾ inches in diameter. Place cookies on a greased baking sheet, slightly apart (they do not spread). Gently press an almond in center of each cooky. Beat the egg yolk with water and brush the mixture over the tops of the cookies.

Bake in a 275° oven for 30 minutes, then increase heat to 350° and bake 10 minutes more or until lightly browned. Carefully remove to wire racks to cool (hot cookies are very fragile). Store airtight. Makes about 3 dozen.

Sweet Bean Buns

Chinese and Japanese stores carry several kinds of canned sweetened bean pastes. Substitute black or yellow bean paste if you can't locate that made from red beans.

These buns can be part of the "Dot-Heart" Lunch described on page 32.

    1   package (amount for two 9-inch crusts)
        pie crust mix
    1   can (about 1 lb. 2 oz.) sweetened red bean paste
        (description on page 14)
    1   egg yolk
    2   tablespoons water

Prepare pastry mix as directed on package for a 2-crust pie. Roll all dough out on a floured board to form a rectangle 12 by 16 inches. Cut in twelve 4-inch squares.

Place an equal amount of the bean paste in each square. Shape bean paste mound in a rectangle about 2 by 2½ inches. Fold short ends of pastry over filling, then lap longer sides over top. *See photograph on opposite page.*

Place seam side down on a greased baking sheet and flatten slightly with your hand. Beat egg yolk with water and brush on each pastry.

Bake in a 375° oven for about 45 minutes or until richly browned. Cool on wire racks. Eat warm or cold. Makes 12.

Preserved Kumquats

The preserved kumquats you buy in bottles are expensive, but these you can make easily are economical.

    4   cups fresh kumquats
        Water
    3   cups each sugar and water

Wash kumquats and remove stems. With a sharp knife, cut a small cross in the blossom end of each fruit. Put kumquats in a large pan with a lid, adding water to cover. Cover pan and bring to boiling; simmer over low heat for 3 minutes.

Drain off water immediately. Put the 3 cups each of sugar and water into pan with kumquats; set over medium heat; bring to boiling, stirring occasionally. Cover and simmer gently for 10 minutes.

If you don't plan to seal the kumquats in canning jars, then set the pan off the heat; leave

SWEET BEAN BUNS (recipe at left) are made by folding dough around sweetened beans you buy canned.

BAKED BUNS are like a turnover. Break them apart and eat out of hand for a snack or for dessert.

lid on and let kumquats cool to room temperature. When cooled, spoon into a quart jar. Covered and refrigerated, they'll keep several weeks.

For longer storage, spoon hot kumquats into hot sterilized pint or half-pint canning jars and cover fruit with hot syrup; adjust lids. Place jars in a rack in a large pan of boiling water; water should cover jars about 1 inch. When water returns to boiling, set timer and boil 5 minutes more; then remove jars from water bath and cool at room temperature. Makes 2 pints.

How to Brew Tea

Chinese teas are like French wines—volumes can be written about them and no one expert is likely to agree with another about their finer points. Connoisseurs each have their own meticulous ways of buying, brewing, and drinking tea.

But perhaps all the Chinese tea experts will agree with this statement: Americans and other English-speaking people brew tea too strong. No matter how great the quality of the tea, if it is too strong it will taste bitter or harsh. Tea of proper strength has a pleasant, natural sweetness.

Test a tea new to you to see what proportion of leaves to water tastes best. This proportion varies with the type of tea and may range from 1 heaping teaspoon of tea leaves per cup of water to only 1 teaspoon for 6 cups of water. A larger measure of big, coarse green tea leaves will be required than of the fine, rolled black tea leaves.

Brew tea this way: Bring water fresh out of the tap just to a brisk boil. Pour some in the teapot to warm it, then pour water out. Add tea to pot and pour the boiling water over it. (For very special teas, the water is cooled somewhat.) Cover and steep at least 3 minutes before serving.

Chinese brew more than one pot of tea from the same leaves. Some believe the second or third brewing is better than the first.

Every kind of tea imaginable is drunk in China. Perhaps there is no such thing as a "Chinese" tea. But certain types are regarded as Chinese in America, such as jasmine tea which contains dried flowers that give sweetness and fragrance.

Many other dried flavorers, such as roses, chrysanthemums, orange blossoms, herbs, and mulberry leaves are added to certain teas. These kinds of things are the *only* flavorers added. Lemon, sugar, and cream are frowned upon.

A JAPANESE RECIPE SAMPLER

A selection of dishes popular with non-natives

Useful information has been included in chapters at the front of this book to help you cook and serve the recipes here.

For a quick survey of principles which apply to all Oriental cooking, read The Essence of an Oriental Art on page 4.

Whenever an unusual ingredient is specified in a recipe, it will be followed with the words "description on page ....." This refers you to the Ingredient Shopping Guide beginning on page 8. There you will find a thorough description of the ingredient and information about where to buy it.

You don't need special equipment for cooking and serving Oriental food. But items you might buy for pleasure are described in Tools and Utensils, How to Use Them, beginning on page 17.

General information about planning meals from these recipes and specific menus based on them are in the chapter called Meal Planning and Party Menus beginning on page 24.

APPETIZERS, PICKLES & SIDE DISHES

The Japanese have a great many classic categories for the appetizers, pickles, side dishes, and soups they serve. These are explained in the section on Japanese Menu and Serving Patterns on page 25. But it will be easier for you to plan a menu if you ignore these categories and judge the dishes in the following section according to American standards. If the dish seems to resemble an appetizer or a salad, serve it that way.

It is more important to plan a balanced, pleasant meal than to be authentic. The recipes in this chapter do not represent all classic categories, but they do offer wide choice.

Many recipes in the main-dish section also can be appetizers. These are Beef, Chicken, Pork

Teriyaki, page 75; Duck Meat Balls, 76; Onigari Yaki, 78; Tempura, pages 76 and 81; and Three Kinds of Sushi, page 84.

Appetizers You Can Buy

You can save yourself much work by buying appetizers which need little or no preparation.

Suitable foods are even available at some supermarkets: Tiny smoked oysters and clams come in cans; just drain and arrange on a plate, or spear with thin skewers. You may find a variety of Japanese crackers called *sembei* or *arare* in cellophane bags. These come in a variety of shapes with a variety of seasonings, including soy sauce, sesame seed, and seaweed. You may also find parched (or fried), salted green peas and beans in bags. Eat these just like nuts.

At gourmet shops you can find boiled and shelled quail eggs, tinted pastel colors, in bottles. Just drain and serve one or two per person.

At Oriental shops there are still other things: You will find plastic bags containing cooked and sweetened red or white beans, or even green peas. The Japanese serve a few of these as appetizers or as side dishes with a meal. You can also buy cooked, frozen soy bean pods (described on page 14) to shell and eat warm or cold.

Sticks of prepared dried cuttlefish tinted red or green (*uni matsuba*) are chewy and much better tasting than you might dream (they resemble beef jerky).

In the canned goods sections you will find these foods which are pretty served on skewers: barbecued mushrooms, fried fish cakes (*tai tempura*), and gingko nuts. Two seafoods come already skewered in the can: broiled octopus on skewers (*tako kushisashi*), which is much more delicious than you might think, and baked white clams on skewers (*yaki hamaguri kushisashi*). All these skewered foods are much improved by a light broiling, just long enough to heat thoroughly. Set up a small hibachi with charcoal and let guests broil their own.

The most beautiful appetizer of all is canned baby abalone in the half shell (*kaitsuki nagareko*). Inch-wide abalone seasoned with soy sauce nestle inside pearly half-shells.

Pickles You Can Buy

At most meals each person is served a tiny dish containing about 1 tablespoon of pungent pickle. At Japanese stores you may buy a great variety of these in plastic bags, cans, or bottles.

The most common kinds are made of cabbage (regular white or celery cabbage) or white radish. The cabbage pickles may be found refrigerated; drain and shred them to serve. The radish pickles, called *takuan*, may be refrigerated or in bottles or cans. If not already sliced, drain and thinly slice them to serve. Most Americans readily like either of these kinds.

Several other more unusual kinds you might enjoy are these (sold in plastic bags): *peaman no yosaburo zuke*, of brilliant green "peaman" cucumber, flavored with ginger; *shizuoka no ume shiso zuke*, of shredded magenta colored ginger, also containing tiny pickled plums and leaves of the beefsteak or *shiso* pepper plant; and *nasu no yosaburozuke*, of eggplant flavored with ginger and soy sauce.

Sashimi

Once you've cultivated a taste for Sashimi (thinly sliced, uncooked fish), you will regard it as the most refreshing dish imaginable. To the initiated, Sashimi is a fine main dish. But unless you're sure of your audience, you might find it wise to offer it as the first course.

The traditional way of serving Sashimi is to arrange rows of the sliced fish on a bed of shredded white radish (*daikon*). A dab of hot green horseradish paste (*wasabi*) is placed on the side. You are given a little sauce dish in which you mix the wasabi with soy sauce for a dip.

If you've never eaten uncooked fish—*really* uncooked, not marinated or dried—you might expect Sashimi to taste fishy. But this isn't so when you buy strictly fresh fish and slice it just before serving. Find out when your fish dealer receives the bulk of his stock, and plan to buy on that day.

The favored fish is tuna; bluefin in summer, yellowfin from time to time during the rest of the year. Both have red flesh. Albacore, which has white flesh, is sometimes used. White sea bass and halibut are other choices. You can arrange the light-colored fish with tuna for contrast.

See photograph of Sashimi on next page.

1 large (about 1 lb.) white radish (daikon, description on page 15), or 3 cups finely shredded cabbage
⅓ small carrot, peeled
1 pound very fresh filleted tuna, white sea bass, or halibut, skinned
  Wasabi Paste or alternate (directions follow)
  Parsley sprig (for garnish)
  Soy sauce

Peel radish and shred into long, fine, grass-like strands. (If your grater doesn't make long strands, use a vegetable peeler to cut the radish lengthwise into paper-thin slices; cut into slivers with a very sharp knife.) The Japanese have special shredders which shred the radish very fine and evenly. See sketch of shredder on page 20.

You should have about 3 cups radish. Shred carrot the same way. Mix shredded radish (or cabbage if used) and carrot; place in ice water.

Quickly rinse fish with cool water; pat dry with paper towels. Cut away and discard any dark portions (in red-fleshed fish, these will be almost black). If fish is wide, cut lengthwise into 2 or 3 strips (1 to 2-inches wide).

Place fish on cutting board. Using a *very sharp*, thin-bladed knife, start at right and, slicing across the grain, cut fish into ⅛ to ¼-inch slices—the slices should be of uniform size and thickness. To keep the flavor fresh, handle no more than necessary.

(Continued on next page)

SASHIMI (recipe begins on preceding page) is the famous and controversial dish of raw fish. Traditional accompaniments are shredded raw white radish, and zippy green horseradish.

Drain radish-carrot mixture thoroughly and pat dry. Arrange on chilled serving plate. Transfer fish slices with a spatula to serving plate, one row at a time, and arrange over radish, leaving about one-third of the radish exposed on one side of the plate. Japanese custom is to arrange fish in rows with uneven numbers of slices on individual serving dishes. However, you may prefer to prepare one large platter.

Place Wasabi Paste or alternate seasoning at one side of sliced fish. Serve with soy sauce and small sauce dishes for mixing the soy with the Wasabi Paste. Makes 4 servings as a main dish, or 6 servings as an appetizer.

Wasabi Paste. To 4 teaspoons wasabi powder gradually add 4 teaspoons water, blending into a smooth paste. Cover and let stand for about 5 minutes. Description of wasabi is on page 12.

If you can't find wasabi, you can make a paste by blending 4 teaspoons dry mustard with 3 teaspoons water until smooth. Or use about 2 tablespoons prepared horseradish, drained slightly, or grated fresh ginger root.

Steamed Egg Rolls

These rolls have a rim of egg white with yolk filling. They can be eaten with the fingers or with chopsticks by those who have some skill in picking up larger-sized tidbits.

> **8 hard-cooked eggs**
> **Salt**
> **Sugar**

Press whites of the 8 eggs through a fine wire strainer; add ½ teaspoon salt and 2 teaspoons sugar. Press 4 yolks only (use other four yolks for some other purpose such as potato salad or garnish) through fine strainer; add ¼ teaspoon *each* salt and sugar.

Pat out egg white mixture on wet cloth, shaping into neat rectangle 5 by 8 inches. Taper side away from you to a thin edge. *See photograph on page 72.*

Press yolks onto a plate into a 3 by 7-inch rectangle; move by sections with a spatula onto the egg white (*see photograph*), leaving a 1-inch margin at the top and bottom and a ½-inch margin on the sides.

Grasping cloth with the hands, quickly roll the long side of the rectangle to encase yolks, pressing firmly; peel cloth away as you roll. Wrap in cloth, tie ends.

Steam roll 8 to 10 minutes. See information about steamers to buy or improvise and how to use them on page 19.

Chill roll. Unwrap and slice. Makes about 24 slices.

Abalone Goma Zu

This is one of the *sunomono* or vinegared dishes which serves as a relish, salad, or even appetizer —depending on how you choose to regard it. You should make individual servings in small, deep bowls, on small plates, or in the Japanese bowls (small *donburi*) of a shape traditionally used for sunomono dishes. See sketch of bowls for salad-type dishes on page 21.

Goma means sesame and *zu* (or *su*) means vinegar, both used in the dressing.

If you can't find canned abalone, you can substitute cooked crab legs or tiny shrimp.

Garnish each serving bowl as your fancy guides. Sometimes the Japanese use several small garnishes together—such as a parsley leaf, carrot curl, and tomato wedge.

    1   tablespoon sesame seed
    1   tablespoon sugar
    ¼   teaspoon salt
    1   teaspoon cornstarch
    2   tablespoons water or Dashi (instructions
          on page 74)
    ½   cup white vinegar or white rice vinegar
          (described on page 10)
    2   small cucumbers
        Salt
    ½   can (1 lb. size) abalone

Spread sesame seed on a baking sheet and toast in a 350° oven for 5 minutes. Blend the sugar, salt, cornstarch, water or Dashi, and vinegar in a saucepan.

Stirring constantly, simmer until liquid is slightly thick, about 5 minutes. Add sesame seed. Cool.

Peel cucumbers, cut in half lengthwise (removing any large seeds), then cut in thin crosswise slices, and sprinkle with salt. Cut abalone in very thin strips 2 inches long and ½-inch wide. Combine cucumbers and abalone with vinegar mixture. Chill. Serves 4 to 8.

Cucumber Roll

To serve these crab-stuffed rolls as an appetizer, you may either arrange several on individual plates to eat with forks or chopsticks, or place each on a thin cracker or toast round so it can be eaten with the fingers.

    2   large cucumbers
    4   cups water
        Salt
    1   cup (½ lb.) crab meat
    4   hard-cooked egg yolks
    2   tablespoons mayonnaise

Peel cucumbers; discarding ends, cut each in half crosswise. Put into water with 1 tablespoon salt; let stand about 20 minutes. Drain.

Holding each cucumber piece upright and using a sharp knife, cut ⅛-inch thick around full length spirally to center. *See photograph on the next page.*

Discard center. Dry well. Mix the crab meat, egg yolks, mayonnaise, and 1 teaspoon salt. Spread crab mixture on cucumber piece unrolled to lie flat (see photograph). Reroll from center to outside to form pinwheel-type roll.

Chill very well, about 1 hour. Slice ½-inch thick crosswise. Makes about 20 slices.

Cucumber Sunomono (Salad)

For the most authentic flavor, use Japanese vinegar, a mild white rice vinegar which has a very distinctive taste. However, regular white vinegar, diluted a little with water if you like, is perfectly acceptable. The dish won't look right if you substitute amber cider or red wine vinegar.

    2   large cucumbers
    ⅓   cup white vinegar or white rice vinegar
          (description on page 10)
    4   teaspoons sugar
    1   teaspoon salt
    2   slices fresh ginger root, finely chopped
          or slivered

Cut cucumbers in half lengthwise and remove any large seeds; peel if you like. Slice crosswise into very thin slices.

Marinate in a mixture of the vinegar, sugar, salt, and ginger. Chill in the marinade an hour or longer. Makes 6 servings.

EGG ROLL *preparation begins by topping a rectangle of mashed cooked whites with cooked yolks.*

NEXT, EGGS *are rolled up pinwheel fashion. Then the roll will be steamed (recipe on page 70).*

CUCUMBER ROLL *(recipe on preceding page) is made by spreading crab on cucumber strip, rolling up.*

FINISHED ROLLS *are pictured: Cucumber Rolls at left and Steamed Egg Rolls (being sliced) at right.*

Rumaki

This appetizer has become popular in many American restaurants with Oriental, Polynesian, or exotica themes—often listed on the menu under some cooked-up name such as Samurai Special or Eye of the Dragon.

The name Rumaki is Japanese, but the dish may have originated in Hawaii where half the population is Japanese.

¾ pound chicken livers, washed, drained and
     cut in half
1 can (6½ oz.) whole water chestnuts, drained
½ pound bacon
½ cup soy sauce
1 small clove garlic
1 dried hot red chile (about 1-inch long), crushed
6 thin slices fresh ginger root

Fold each piece of liver around a water chestnut, wrap with a half slice bacon, and carefully fasten with wooden picks or bamboo skewers.

Mix together the soy sauce, garlic, chile, and ginger. Marinate the chicken liver bundles in this sauce for several hours, turning occasionally.

Then place the appetizers on a rack in a shallow pan and broil 5 to 7 minutes, turning once. Serve hot. (Or use an hibachi with charcoal to broil or reheat the Rumaki.) Makes about 18.

Triangle Eggs

Many of the Japanese garnishes are doubly beautiful because they reflect an ingenious streak as well as artistic flair—such as these eggs cooked to a triangular shape in paper cones. Use them to garnish Clear Soup, recipe on this page.

Cut 8-inch squares of bond paper or paper bags (bond works best; foil is not satisfactory). Oil the papers with salad oil.

Fold each square in half diagonally, forming a triangle; then again, forming a smaller triangle. Open each to form a pocket and break a small egg into it. Stand the paper cones up in a small, deep pan of boiling water, so that the point is at the bottom, the opening at the top. (If you wish, fasten the papers together with a paper clip.) Water should come up to the top of the eggs.

Keep water just under a boil and cook the eggs 6 to 10 minutes, or until all the white is set. Spoon some simmering water into the top of each egg if top does not set as soon as the rest. Drain and carefully peel off paper; trim off ragged edges.

Clear Soup (Suimono)

This is served in individual bowls containing just a few tiny bits of colorful foods for garnish. The clarity of the soup and the beauty of the garnishes indicate the skill of a cook.

The soup is easy to make and any number of things you have on hand may serve as garnish. Dashi broth is most typical, but you can substitute chicken.

3 cups regular-strength chicken broth or Dashi
     (instructions on page 74)
1½ teaspoons soy sauce
     Salt to taste
     Garnishes (suggestions follow)

Prepare Dashi and pour in a deep bottle; let stand undisturbed 30 minutes for sediment to settle; carefully pour off the clear liquid and use that in the bottom for other cooking.

Heat the broth with the soy sauce and salt to taste, just to a simmer. Serve in small, individual bowls, each containing your choice of garnishes. The soup is sipped from the bowl (usually the Japanese type sketched on page 21). Garnishes, particularly large ones, may then be picked up and eaten with chopsticks. Serves 4.

Garnishes. The garnishes should offer contrast in shape, texture, and color. One of them can be some substantial food of one or two-bite size, but the rest are very small and delicate. Use just one piece of each thing per bowl. Three different garnishes per bowl are attractive.

Some things of a delicate "leafy" nature are a parsley leaf, watercress sprig, celery leaf, or tiny spinach leaf. A piece of green onion top, green bean, or celery stalk can be slivered at one end to resemble a spray of pine needles. Green onion tops can also be thinly sliced crosswise.

One of the items may be a small slice—of water chestnut, carrot, bamboo shoot, mushroom, or lemon peel. These can also be cut in decorative shapes with a tiny cutter, or they can be diced.

Another item might be long and thin—such as a piece of cooked noodle, or a strip of any of the preceding foods for slicing.

Some more substantial foods might be a whole cooked shrimp, a cooked oyster or clam (in half-shell perhaps), a cube of fresh soy bean cake (*tofu*, described on page 14), a strip of cooked chicken, a slice of abalone, or a slice of steamed fish cake (*kamaboko*, described on page 12).

Triangle Eggs also make an attractive substantial garnish, (recipe on this page).

Miso Soup with Egg

Many soups are made from a thick fermented soy bean paste called *miso*, which comes in two forms—white and red—described on page 11.

In fact, Japanese soups are classified by names indicating whether they are clear broth soups (*suimono*) or contain miso (*misoshiru*).

The flavor of miso can't be compared to anything in American cuisine, but still most people like it at once, particularly the white kind.

Following is a recipe for making the soup from scratch. But if you want to save time, you can buy foil packets of either white or red miso soup mix· at Japanese stores. These have directions in English.

Some canned miso soups are also marketed, ready to heat and eat. A particularly intriguing version of red miso is labelled *Karatsuki Shijimi-Misojiru* (shiru). It contains many pea-sized brown shijimi clams in their tiny brown-and-white shells.

    4 cups regular-strength chicken or beef broth
        or Dashi (instructions below)
    ¼ cup fermented soy bean paste (white miso,
        description on page 11)
    ¼ teaspoon salt
    1 egg, beaten
    2 teaspoons sherry or sweet rice wine, optional
        (description on page 10)
        Twists of orange or lemon peel and slices of
        green onion tops for garnish

Bring broth or Dashi mixed with miso and salt to a boil. While swirling the soup in the pan, gradually trickle in the beaten egg. Remove from heat. Add wine, if you wish.

Place a twist of orange or lemon peel in each bowl before adding soup. Top with green onion rings. Serves 4 to 6.

Dashi (Broth)

Dashi is a broth made of dried bonito fish (*katsuobushi*) and dried tangle seaweed (*kombu*). It is used for soup, sauces, and the cooking liquid for many simmered dishes.

Dashi is the one ingredient that gives Japanese food its most characteristic flavor, a flavor that some foreigners don't like but which others come to relish. Dashi is clear and light in flavor. Chicken broth or fish broth, therefore, make good substitutes.

At Japanese markets you can buy the ingredients to make Dashi from scratch. But the easiest way to prepare it is to buy packages labelled "Dashi-no-Moto soup stock." These come in two forms—bags like tea bags containing the ingredients, or pellets like bouillon cubes. Most of these packages give you instructions in English for brewing the Dashi.

To make it with the tea-bag type, you just drop one ¾ oz. bag in 3 cups of boiling water and simmer about 5 minutes. Remove the bag (don't mash it or the broth will be cloudy) and you have Dashi. Some taste testers report that they prefer the flavor of this instant Dashi to the type made from scratch.

VARIED SEAFOOD & MEAT MAIN DISHES

Teriyaki dishes are appreciated by almost all Americans, hence several are included here.

Fish Teriyaki

Japanese love whole fish broiled over charcoal, but the fish fillets used in this recipe are easier to handle in your oven broiler.

    1 cup soy sauce
    ½ cup sugar
    ¼ cup salad oil
    2 teaspoons grated fresh ginger root
    1 clove garlic, chopped (optional)
    2 to 3 pounds rockfish fillets (often called
        rock cod, sea bass, red snapper, or Pacific
        Ocean perch)
    1 tablespoon sesame seed
        Shredded lettuce (optional)

In a bowl, combine soy sauce, sugar, oil, ginger, and garlic, if used. Let fillets stand in this mixture for several hours.

Line a shallow baking pan with aluminum foil. Lift fillets from soy sauce mixture and arrange in pan. Broil 5 to 7 inches from heat for about 4 minutes, brushing once or twice with a little additional oil. Turn, brush with more oil, and sprinkle with sesame seed. Broil 3 to 5 minutes longer, or until fish flakes. Serve on a bed of shredded lettuce, if you like. Makes 4 to 6 servings.

Chicken Teriyaki

You can serve this soy-seasoned chicken at least two ways: It can be a hot or cold appetizer to eat with the fingers, or a main dish.

2½ to 3-pound broiler-fryer chicken, cut up
¾ cup soy sauce
¼ cup sugar
¼ cup dry sherry or white rice wine (sake, description on page 10)
2 teaspoons grated fresh ginger root
1 small clove garlic, crushed

Wash chicken quickly in cool water and pat dry with paper towels. Using a meat cleaver or heavy knife to cut through bones with a single, carefully aimed blow, cut thighs and legs into 2 pieces *each*. Cut halved breasts into 3 pieces each. Discard wing tips, and cut remainder of each wing in two. Cut back into 4 or 5 pieces.

Place cut chicken in a shallow bowl. Pour on Teriyaki marinade made by blending all the remaining ingredients. Cover and refrigerate for 2 to 3 hours, turning occasionally.

Drain chicken, reserving marinade. Place pieces, skin sides down, in a single layer in a greased 9 by 13-inch baking pan. Bake in a 450° oven for 10 minutes.

Turn chicken; bake for 10 minutes more. Reduce oven temperature to 350°; pour off and discard pan liquid. Continue baking for 30 minutes longer, or until tender, brushing 2 or 3 times with some of the reserved marinade.

Broil about 6 inches from heat for 3 minutes, or until chicken is well browned. Serve with some pan drippings poured over if you like. Makes 4 servings as a main dish, or 6 to 8 as an appetizer.

Beef Teriyaki

The sauce for all the *teriyaki* ("glaze-broiled") dishes contains soy sauce, some kind of sweetening, and almost always ginger and garlic.

You may add red or white wine, sherry, or the Japanese wines, *sake* or *mirin*, described on page 10. Cut back on the sugar used if the wine is sweet.

A small amount of tomato flavoring, such as a tablespoon of chile sauce, catsup, or tomato paste is good. A crushed red chile or a dash of liquid hot-pepper seasoning adds zest. Onion juice, lemon juice, or lime juice can also be used.

You can always garnish the broiled meat with toasted sesame seed (whole, crushed, or ground).

2 pounds boneless, tender beef steak
1¾ cups soy sauce
½ cup sugar
½ teaspoon crushed garlic
1 tablespoon grated fresh ginger root, or
2 tablespoons minced preserved or candied ginger

Cut meat into 4 pieces and place in a bowl. In a pan combine the soy sauce, sugar, garlic, and ginger. Heat just until sugar is dissolved; cool. Pour mixture over meat and marinate for 1 hour.

Remove meat from marinade and grill over glowing coals, or broil in your oven until done to your liking. (Leftover marinade keeps well in the refrigerator for several weeks.) Slice each piece into finger-sized pieces. Makes 4 servings.

Pork Teriyaki

See the recipe for Beef Teriyaki for possible flavor variations in the marinade.

2 pounds boneless pork steak, cut in 1-inch cubes
1 cup soy sauce
¼ cup sherry or sweet rice wine (mirin, described on page 10)
1 clove garlic, crushed
1 teaspoon sugar

Marinate meat for 1 hour in a mixture of the soy sauce, sherry, crushed garlic, and sugar.

Broil slowly, basting with the marinade during broiling. Serves 4.

(If you wish to barbecue the pork over charcoal, cut it into serving-sized pieces, then after broiling cut in finger-sized slices.)

Chawan Mushi

You can buy special little covered dishes used for making these fragile, main-dish custards. The covers keep steam from dripping into the custards as you cook them and keep them hot until serving time. At a Japanese store, they will know what you mean if you ask for Chawan Mushi dishes (sketched on page 21).

Although the special dishes are attractive, you don't have to get them. Custard cups or individual casseroles can be used.

    1   can (5 oz.) boned chicken, cut in small pieces
    2   tablespoons soy sauce
    12 cooked shrimp, peeled and deveined
    1½ cups of 1-inch pieces watercress or spinach
    6   large mushrooms, cut in half
    6   thin slices lemon
    3½ cups regular-strength chicken broth or Dashi
        (instructions on page 74)
    1½ cups eggs (about 8), well beaten
    ¼   teaspoon salt

Mix together chicken and soy sauce. Place in each of 6 cups (1½-cup size) an equal amount of chicken, shrimp, watercress, mushrooms, and lemon. Fill with broth beaten with eggs and salt.

Set cups in a large shallow pan of hot water over direct heat (water should be deep enough to come halfway up sides of cups), and lay a baking sheet over cups to cover if cups have no lids.

Poach in hot—not boiling—water until custard is firm in the center when dish is shaken; this takes 25 to 30 minutes. Serve hot. Serves 6.

Duck Meat Balls

These elegant ground duck meat balls may be either a main dish or appetizers.

    4   to 5-pound duck
    3   tablespoons soy sauce
    1   tablespoon dry sherry or white rice wine (sake, description on page 10)

Cut the duck meat from the bone, discarding most of the fat. Grind the meat in the food chopper or mince very fine with a heavy cleaver.

Mix the ground duck with soy sauce and wine until thoroughly blended. Chill about 1 hour, or until mixture is stiff enough to handle. Form into balls about 1 inch in diameter and thread on thin skewers.

Flatten balls slightly, then broil over hot coals until brown on both sides. (Brown the balls well on one side before you turn them over, so they won't fall off the skewers.) Serves 4 as a main dish, 8 to 10 as appetizers.

Curried Chicken Tempura

This version of crisp-fried Tempura is made with inexpensive chicken wings cut a special way.

    2   dozen broiler-fryer chicken wings
    ½   egg
    10 tablespoons water
    6   tablespoons cornstarch
    6   tablespoons regular all-purpose flour
    1   teaspoon salt
    2   teaspoons each sugar and curry powder
        About 2 quarts salad oil for deep-frying
        Soy sauce or Tempura Sauce (recipe on page 82)

Cut the chicken wings off at the first joint and use just the large first section (the wing tips and center sections can be used for making broth).

Start at the small end of each large wing piece, and with a sharp knife cut the meat from the bone down to the end, leaving the meat attached to the bone at the large end. Pat excess moisture from wings with paper towels.

For the batter, break one egg into a measuring cup, beat with a fork, pour half into a small bowl (save other half for some other use); add water, cornstarch, flour, salt, sugar, and curry powder. Mix just until well blended. Set the bowl inside a bowl of cracked ice.

PINE NEEDLE TEMPURA (recipe below) is made by dipping noodles in batter, then holding in hot oil.

NOODLE SPRAY after cooking looks just like pine needles, but is very crunchy and good to eat.

To cook Tempura at the table (preferably out of doors), use an electric frying pan, deep-fat fryer with a good heat regulator, fondue pan, or *Tempura nabe* over an hibachi (see sketch on page 20).

Set pan on a side table or tea cart (there may be some spattering of fat as you fry). Nearby arrange the prepared chicken wings, the batter in a bowl with ice, a cake rack over a shallow pan for draining the cooked food, and a slotted spoon, tongs, or a Japanese screen-wire skimmer for removing food from the oil (sketched on page 20).

Heat the salad oil (about 1½ inches deep) in the pan to a temperature between 350° and 355°. If possible, use a deep-fat-frying thermometer. Hold each chicken wing by the bone and dip into the batter, drain briefly, then put into the hot fat. Cook until golden brown, turning several times (takes about 2 to 3 minutes). Lift out with a slotted spoon and drain briefly.

Don't cook more than 4 or 5 pieces at one time or the fat will cool too much. (If you use a fondue pan, cook only 2 or 3 at one time.) Skim off any drops of batter that form in the fat so they won't burn and flavor the oil. Pass soy sauce at the table or have dishes of Tempura Sauce ready. Makes about 4 servings.

"Pine Needles" Garnish For Tempura

Intriguing shapes that resemble clusters of long pine needles are made of thin, vermicelli-like noodles while you are preparing Tempura (recipes on the opposite page and page 81).

See photographs above.

> Uncooked very thin, round noodles such as somen (description on page 9)
> Tempura batter (with Tempura recipes)
> Oil for deep frying

Take a little bunch of the noodles (about ¼ inch in diameter), and break to make needles about 3 inches long. Holding the bunch firmly together, dip about ¼-inch of the end into the batter, then hold this end in the hot oil (about 350°) while you count 5 seconds (this will fuse the noodles together at the end).

Then simply let go so the needles drop into the oil. They will spread immediately and will begin to brown rather quickly. Remove them as soon as they are lightly browned, in about a minute.

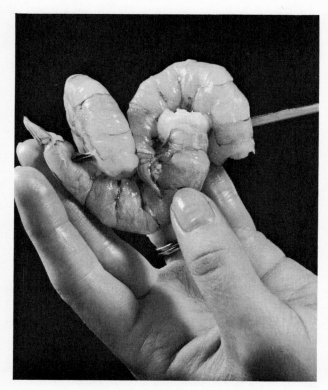

ONIGARI YAKI, the broiled shrimp dish below, is most beautiful if shrimp are skewered in this fashion.

Onigari Yaki

In Japan shrimp for this dish are threaded on bamboo skewers in a fancy serpentine design. The design pattern is not necessary, but definitely worth the extra trouble.

This could be classified as a *teriyaki* ("glaze-broiled") dish. It is most delicious cooked over charcoal, but you could prepare it under an oven broiler.

½   cup sherry or sweet rice wine (mirin, description on page 10)
1   cup soy sauce
1   tablespoon sugar
36   large raw shrimp (about 3 lbs.), peeled and deveined

In a small saucepan, combine wine, soy sauce, and sugar; bring to a boil.

Thread 6 shrimp on each skewer. *See photograph above.*

Dip skewers in sauce and then broil over hot coals. Brush constantly with sauce until shrimp are glazed and barely tender, just a few minutes broiling on each side. Makes 6 servings.

DISHES WHICH SERVE AS A COMPLETE MEAL

Almost any guest will enjoy the following four dishes which comprise a full meal.

Kabuto Yaki

This meat and vegetable meal of Mongolian origin can be cooked over an hibachi with a special dome that fits on top. According to one account, the first domes were soldiers' helmets; Genghis Khan's warriors wore metal hats with slits in them, and used them as cooking grills. The word *kabuto* means "helmet." For information about the Genghis Khan grill, see page 22.

If you don't have a dome, you can prepare this dish on any barbecue or hibachi, using "expanded steel," welded hardware cloth, or a broiler rack over the grill to keep the small pieces of food from falling through.

A menu featuring the dish appears on page 27 and *the meal being prepared is photographed on page 31.*

1½   pounds boneless beef steak
1½   pounds boneless pork shoulder
10   green onions
3   zucchini
1   eggplant
½   pound green beans, parboiled about 5 minutes
¼   pound edible-pod peas (described on page 14)
½   pound mushrooms
     Salad oil or sesame oil (optional)
     Goma (Sesame) Sauce (recipe follows)

Cut both beef and pork in very thin slices, about like bacon, and about 2 by 3 inches.

Cut green onions in 2½-inch lengths, including some of the green tops. Cut zucchini and eggplant in 2½-inch "fingers" about ¼-inch thick. Cut beans in 2½-inch pieces. String pea pods and leave whole. Cut mushrooms lengthwise in slices ¼-inch thick.

To cook, start with the pieces of pork, setting them on the rounded part of the dome over glowing coals. Next, add the beef, cooking it just a minute or two, or until done to your liking. As the meat juices and fat collect along the edge of the dome, place the vegetables in this liquid and let simmer until done (usually they are eaten fairly crisp).

If you don't use a dome, vegetables and meat may be dipped in oil before being placed on the grill.

Small bowls of the Goma Sauce—one for each person—should be provided for dunking the hot meat and vegetables after they are cooked. Use tongs, cooking forks, or chopsticks to lift and turn the meat and vegetables. Makes 6 servings.

Goma (Sesame) Sauce. Toast 1 cup sesame seed in a dry frying pan over medium heat, stirring to brown evenly. Grind the seeds to a paste with an electric blender or in a Japanese *suribachi*, sketched on page 20.

Blend in thoroughly 1 cup soy sauce, 1 cup water, 1 puréed clove of garlic, 1 tablespoon sugar, ½ cup white vinegar, ½ cup sherry or white rice wine (*sake*), and 1 large unpeeled apple, grated. Make this several days ahead so the flavors will blend. Makes about 3½ cups.

Mizutaki Dinner

For this lean but satisfying dish which is also a whole meal, you cook bite-sized morsels of meat and vegetables in simmering broth at the dinner table, then dip them in sauce. For the finale, ladle the well-flavored broth into sauce bowls which still contain a little sauce to make a soup.

The traditional cooking pot is the vessel popularly called a "hot pot," and known in Japan as a Mizutaki or Shabu Shabu pot.

For instructions about different kinds of pots which can be used at the table, see Cook-at-the-Table equipment, page 19.

For information about how to present this dish as a party meal, see the Japanese Mizutaki Dinner menu on page 30. *The dish is photographed on page 28.*

> Boneless Meat (instructions follow)
> Raw Vegetables (instructions follow)
> Mizutaki Sauce or Sesame Sauce (recipes follow)
> Condiments (optional)
> About 2 quarts lightly seasoned, regular-strength beef or chicken broth

Prepare meat, vegetables, sauces, and condiments (if used) according to instructions following.

At each place provide a bowl of the Mizutaki Sauce, plate, chopsticks or fork, and a teacup.

Just before you ask the diners to be seated, bring the broth to boiling on the kitchen range and then pour enough into the cooking pot to fill it 2 to 3 inches deep; keep the rest of the broth simmering to replenish the pot during second and third cookings.

While still in the kitchen, put into the pot a selection of the items needing longest cooking (chicken, carrots, cauliflower, green onions, leeks, mushrooms), keeping each kind together in a separate area of the broth as much as possible. Cover and simmer about 5 minutes.

After guests are seated, bring the cooking pot to the table. Then add beef, bean cake, and spinach. After 2 or 3 minutes more of cooking (with the cover on) serve a selection of all the cooked foods to each guest.

Fill the cooker again while the first servings are eaten.

For a more leisurely meal, furnish each person with cooking chopsticks or little wire ladles and let each do his own cooking. Ladles are sketched on page 20.

Toward the end of the dinner, ladle some of the cooking broth into each person's sauce bowl to be stirred into the sauce left in the bowl; sip like a soup. Serves 6.

Boneless Meat. Use 1½ pounds boneless beef sirloin, cut 1½ to 2 inches thick, and 6 chicken thighs. Thinly slice the beef across the grain. Bone and skin chicken and cut meat in 1-inch pieces or thinly slice. You could substitute any lean, tender beef steak or chicken breasts.

Instead of the beef and chicken, you might use lean pork such as pork tenderloin or thick pork chops (bone and fat removed), thinly sliced as for beef. Or use any cut of lean boneless lamb, cut like beef.

Partially freeze meats to cut in thin, neat slices

Raw Vegetables. Use 1 bunch carrots, peeled and thinly sliced; 1 small head cauliflower, cut into small flowerettes; 1 bunch *each* green onions and leeks, cut in 2-inch pieces; ½ pound mushrooms, sliced; 1 bunch fresh spinach (tender, small leaves); ½ pound fresh soy bean cake (*tofu*), cubed, described on page 14.

Here are suggestions for additions or substitutions: dried mushrooms, soaked in water until soft, sliced with stems removed; fresh asparagus cut in 2-inch pieces; broccoli flowerettes; whole edible-pod peas; celery cabbage broken into pieces or sliced in rounds; watercress sprigs; sliced bamboo shoots; sliced water chestnuts; green pepper strips. Special vegetables and mushrooms are described on pages 14-16.

Mizutaki Sauce. This is very similar to a sauce served in a San Francisco Japanese restaurant. In a blender combine 1 egg, 2 tablespoons white vinegar, ¼ teaspoon dry mustard, and ¼ cup salad oil; whirl until blended.

(Continued on next page)

With blender motor on high, gradually add ¾ cup more oil in a slow steady stream. Whirl about 30 seconds more, then pour into a bowl. (Or substitute 1¼ cups bottled mayonnaise for this homemade version.)

Stir in ⅓ cup sour cream, 2 tablespoons soy sauce, 2 tablespoons sherry or sweet rice wine (mirin), ⅓ cup regular-strength beef or chicken broth, and 1 teaspoon sesame oil (optional). Mirin and sesame oil are described on page 10.

Refrigerate until serving time. Makes 1¼ cups, enough for 6 servings.

Sesame Sauce. This sauce is based on one served by a Kyoto restaurant.

Toast 1 cup sesame seed in a dry frying pan over medium heat, stirring to brown evenly. Grind until fine and slightly pasty in consistency (use high speed in an electric blender, or grind a few at a time with a mortar and pestle such as the *suribachi* sketched on page 20).

Thoroughly blend with ½ cup sesame oil or salad oil, ½ cup soy sauce, 2 tablespoons white vinegar or lemon juice, and ¾ cup beef broth or water. Makes about 2 cups sauce.

Condiments. These are all optional, but are nice to have on the table for each guest to add to his bowl of sauce: finely minced green onions, grated fresh ginger root, and Japanese chile powder mixture, *togarashi,* described on page 10.

East-West Sukiyaki

This is called East-West because you can use your choice of Western (American) ingredients available at any market or can incorporate as many Eastern (Oriental) foods as you can find.

Legend says that Sukiyaki was originated by farmers who cooked the dish in the fields in the metal part of their ploughs (*suki* means plough and *yaki* means broiled). Obviously such a dish would use whatever ingredients were handy or growing nearby. Therefore, having a wide choice of foods to use is completely in keeping with the spirit of the original dish.

Nevertheless, you will find such modern equipment as electric frying pans or hot plates best for "plough-broiling" indoors at the table. For information about Sukiyaki pans and other cook-at-the-table equipment, see page 19.

Although Sukiyaki has come a long way, it still serves the original purpose of providing an easy, complete meal cooked in the presence of those who eat it and served from one pan.

1   or 2-inch cube of beef suet, cut in 4 pieces
2   pounds boneless, tender beef steak (such as tenderloin or sirloin), trimmed of fat and cut in paper-thin slices 1 by 2 inches
2   small onions, cut in ¼-inch slices, then each slice cut in half
12   to 16 green onions including tops, or 6 leeks trimmed of all green and split lengthwise; cut onions or leeks in 1½-inch lengths
½   pound medium-sized mushrooms, or 1 can (15 oz.) straw mushrooms, drained (description on page 16)
4   or 5 stalks celery, or ½ small head celery cabbage (description on page 15)
1   pound spinach, or ½ to 1 pound garland chrysanthemum (description on page 15)
4   ounces thin spaghetti, or thin translucent noodles (description on page 9)
3-egg omelet, cooked and cooled, or ½ pound fresh soy bean cake (description on page 14)
4   to 6 uncooked eggs for dipping sauce (optional) Sukiyaki Broth (two recipes follow)

To prepare and present ingredients, cut and arrange ingredients as directed following. Arrange each food separately, side by side, on large trays or flat baskets. Cover and refrigerate until ready to cook. If you plan to serve the eggs as sauce, break each into a small cup and beat to blend. Pour Sukiyaki Broth into a pitcher.

The suet, beef, onions, and green onions are to be used whether the Sukiyaki is "East" or "West."

Cut fresh mushrooms through stems in ¼-

inch-thick slices; cut straw mushrooms in half lengthwise.

Cut celery diagonally ¼-inch thick; cut celery cabbage crosswise ½-inch thick.

Discard stems of spinach or chrysanthemum leaves, and use tender leaves only.

Cook spaghetti in boiling, unsalted water until barely tender, drain, and cover with cold water; drain to use. Cover translucent noodles with cold water for 30 minutes to 1 hour, drain, and wrap well (no need to cook).

Cut omelet in ½-inch squares; cut bean cake in ½-inch cubes.

To cook Sukiyaki (either in kitchen or at table), heat a 10-inch Sukiyaki pan or frying pan over medium-high heat on the range or a portable electric heat unit; or use an electric frying pan. Prepare the Sukiyaki in two portions, half of each ingredient at a time. Keep each type of food together in one section of the pan during cooking.

Stir suet in pan until pan is well coated with fat; remove browned suet. Stir half the beef in pan until it loses pinkness, then push into a corner of the pan. Add half of both kinds of onions (reserving green tops) and cook, turning frequently until beginning to brown; turn mound of meat occasionally.

Place half the fresh mushrooms in one area of the pan and half the celery in another. Add about half the Sukiyaki Broth (either style) and simmer uncovered about 5 minutes; turn all foods occasionally. (If you use straw mushrooms and celery cabbage, add later and cook about 2 minutes.)

Push each food aside separately and add half the spinach or chrysanthemum and green onion tops, pushing them down into liquid and turning frequently; when wilted, push into a mound.

Add the spaghetti or noodles and bean cake, pushing other foods aside to make room for them. Turn to heat and absorb broth. If you use the fragile omelet squares, just heat lightly.

To serve, turn heat to low. Dish up servings into bowls or plates, or let guests help themselves from the cooking pan. Those who like may dip each bite into the beaten egg sauce.

When the pan is empty, pour out any remaining broth and repeat the cooking with the other half of each ingredient. Makes 4 to 6 servings.

Western-Style Sukiyaki Broth. Stir together ½ cup soy sauce, 2 tablespoons sugar, ¼ cup dry sherry, ½ cup regular-strength beef broth, and ¼ cup water.

Japanese-Style Sukiyaki Broth. Stir together ½ cup soy sauce, 2 tablespoons sugar, ¼ cup white rice wine (saki, described on page 10), and ¾ cup Dashi (instructions on page 74).

Seafood-Vegetable Tempura

To make a whole dinner party of these crisp seafood and vegetable "fritters," see the Japanese Tempura Party menu on page 26.

But there is no need to reserve Tempura for entertaining. Accompanied with a bowl of steamed rice, it can provide a varied and nutritious meal whenever you buy any kind of seafood. It can also be appetizers.

> **Fish and shellfish** (see following suggestions)
> **Vegetables** (see following suggestions)
> **Batter** (see following recipe)
> **Fresh, bland salad oil for deep frying** (use part sesame oil if available)
> **Tempura Sauce** (see following recipe)
> **"Pine Needles" Garnish**, optional, (recipe on page 77)

Preparation of equipment is essential to making good Tempura. The heat of the oil is very important, so an electric frying pan or deep fat fryer is probably most satisfactory.

A *Tempura nabe* (special pan with rack on side described on page 18) may be more dramatic, and is very convenient, too, if you use it over an electric hot plate that has several heat settings or an hibachi that has good draft control.

Have ready a cake rack on a shallow pan or tray for draining the pieces (unless you have a *Tempura nabe*).

Dip the prepared food into the batter, holding it by tail or stem, or with chopsticks or tongs. Let it drip a second, then put into the hot fat (350° to 375° is best). Cook until golden brown.

It is wise to turn the foods a few seconds after they are put into the fat; this makes subsequent turning easier. You'll need two sets of chopsticks or other holders; leave one in the batter, and use the other to lift foods out of the fat. Skim out the drops of batter so they won't burn.

Do not cook too much food at one time or it will cool the fat too fast. If the temperature drops below 350°, the food will absorb oil and not be crisp. Put in first the foods that must cook longer, such as shrimp; add those like spinach last.

To eat, dip each piece in the sauce. *See photograph on next page.*

Fish and Shellfish. Allow ¾ pound per person for a full meal. Do not precook; dry well.

Select from the following: *Crab*, shell and keep in chunks; *fish*, cut boneless pieces small enough to eat in one or two bites, but leave small fish such as whitebait whole (remove heads); *lobster*

CRISP TEMPURA (recipe begins on preceding page) may be served in napkin-lined baskets. Dipping sauces or condiments are traditionally presented in individual dishes on the side.

tails, shell and cut in slices across the grain; *oysters and clams,* drain well and cut in half if large; *scallops,* cut in half if large; *shrimp,* remove shells but leave tails on, devein; split almost through the vein side, spread flat, and score lightly with cross-hatch pattern to prevent curling when they cook.

Vegetables. Allow ½ to ¾ pound (total) per person for a full meal. Dry thoroughly. Select from the following: *Asparagus,* cut in 1-inch diagonal slices; *carrots* and *celery,* cut in thin, diagonal slices; *eggplant,* cut in ¼-inch slices and quarter; *green beans,* boil 5 minutes, drain, and cut in 2-inch lengths; *green onions,* cut in 1 to 2-inch lengths; *fresh mushrooms,* use whole if small or slice; *spinach,* use small leaves with all but ½-inch of stem removed; *summer squash,* cut in ½-inch slices; *sweet potatoes,* peel and thinly slice; *watercress,* break in small branches.

You can also use several exotic vegetables: *fresh lotus root,* peel and thinly slice, described on page 16; *Chinese parsley,* break into branches, described on page 11; or *shungiku,* tear leaves off the stems, described on page 15; *edible-pod peas,* remove tips and "string," described on page 14.

Batter. Combine 2 eggs with 15 tablespoons (1 cup minus 1 tablespoon) cold water; beat until frothy. Beat in ¾ cup unsifted flour (also add ½ teaspoon salt for Occidental palates) until blended—don't beat the flour any more than is necessary. Set the bowl of batter inside another bowl with ice, to keep it cold.

Sauce. Some may prefer Tempura served simply, with quartered lemon and salt. The Japanese always have a sauce, made of the fish and seaweed broth, *Dashi,* recipe on page 74.

To make sauce, combine in a pan 3 cups prepared Dashi or fish stock; 1 cup soy sauce; and 1 cup rice wine (sake), sherry, or sweet rice wine (mirin), described on page 10.

Bring to a boil, and remove from heat. Serve hot in little individual bowls. Makes enough for 6 people.

Besides the sauce, provide each guest with a small dish of grated white Oriental radish (daikon) and/or grated fresh ginger root. (If the daikon is not available, substitute 2 parts grated red radish and 1 part grated turnip.) Or mix either the radish or ginger into the hot sauce. The radish is described on page 15.

RICE, NOODLES & SUSHI RICE DISHES

Rice and noodles are the staffs of Japanese life and appear in some form with every meal.

Noodles

For information about all the various types of Oriental noodles, read the section about them on pages 8 and 9.

Japanese love to make a whole light meal out of noodles in hot broth, often topped with substantial cooked foods.

The easiest way, quickest, and most inexpensive way to sample several kinds of noodles prepared in broth is to buy a modern innovation, called "instant" noodles.

Instant noodles are partially cooked and then dried in blocks. They come in little cellophane packages of about 3 ounces containing the noodle block, a foil packet of dry soup stock base, and sometimes dried onion or spice. One package makes a whole-meal serving for one person and costs about 20 cents.

Most of these packages have instructions in English. Here is how you usually prepare these:

Bring 1½ to 3 cups of water to a boil (best to start with 1½ cups and add more later if you think the soup stock is too strong). Drop in the block of noodles, which will begin to soften immediately. Add the contents of the foil soup-stock-base packet. Stir to dissolve and to separate the noodles. Simmer only 2 or 3 minutes. The noodles are done.

If you like, top with some of these cooked foods: whole shrimp, pieces of chicken or barbecued pork, abalone slices, hard-cooked egg slices, whole canned mushrooms, bamboo shoot slices, whole edible-pod peas, carrot slices, and steamed fish cake slices (kamaboko, see description on page 12).

You can always add sliced green onion tops.

Some of these noodle packages are labelled "instant noodles," but most are not. Some of the label names you will see are: ramen (white curled noodles); tanmen; rai-rai ken; yaki soba; miso ramen (containing miso bean paste); tanuki curry udon (curry-flavored wide white noodles); jindaiji or tanuki soba (brown buckwheat noodles); ebis wantan men (curled white noodles plus dried Chinese-type won ton which also cook soft in 2 minutes); and chuka bifun (thin translucent Chinese-style rice noodles).

Rice with Peas

The Chinese are not the only ones who prepare fried rice. The people of any rice-eating country are likely to make such a dish because it is such a good way to use up leftovers.

- ½ cup salad oil, butter, or margarine
- ½ cup sliced green onion, including some of the green tops
- ¼ cup minced parsley
- 1 package (10 oz.) frozen peas
  Boiling, salted water
- 4 cups cooked rice, hot or cold (about 1⅓ cups rice before cooking)
- 2 teaspoons grated lemon peel
- 2 tablespoons soy sauce
  Dash liquid hot-pepper seasoning

In a frying pan, heat the oil; add green onion and parsley and sauté just until limp and bright green, about 3 minutes.

Meanwhile add peas to boiling water and bring just back to boiling; remove from heat, drain, and set aside.

Add the rice, lemon peel, soy sauce, hot-pepper seasoning, and peas to the frying pan. Stir over heat, being careful not to mash rice grains, until heated through. Makes 4 to 6 servings.

Japanese Rice

The secret of Japanese rice, which clings together so it is easy to pick up with chopsticks, is the use of short or medium-grain rice, proper water measurement, and "no-peek" covered cooking.

If you time the cooking exactly as the recipe says, the rice will turn out just right.

- 1 cup short or medium-grain rice (described on page 8)
- 1¼ cups cold water
- ½ teaspoon salt (optional)

Put rice in a heavy, deep pan which has a tight-fitting lid or the special saucepan for cooking rice sketched on page 20.

Add cold water and salt (Japanese don't use it), cover, and soak for 1 to 2 hours.

(Note: The Japanese usually wash the rice thoroughly before soaking, but this is not necessary unless you buy rice in bulk which is coated with talc. Washing removes vitamins.)

(Continued on next page)

Set covered pan over high heat and bring quickly to a full boil. Reduce heat to *lowest* setting and let rice simmer exactly 12 minutes for 1 to 3 cups rice, 15 minutes if more is used. Turn off heat and let rice stand 5 minutes or longer.

Never take the lid off during cooking. It is best not to remove the lid until ready to serve. Makes 4 or 5 servings.

Three Kinds of Sushi

Sushi serves the same purpose as a sandwich. It is a cold dish (of slightly sweet-and-sour rice) which can usually be eaten with the fingers, can be made ahead, and is convenient to carry in a lunch box. It also is eaten like a sandwich, as a snack, appetizer, or lunch—seldom for dinner. However, it also can be dressed up and served as elegantly as a "club sandwich special."

There are three main kinds of Sushi: Those called *nigiri zushi,* consist of rice balls topped with various ingredients such as fish or shrimp. Those called *norimaki zushi* consist of rice and an assortment of colorful ingredients rolled pinwheel fashion inside a wrapping such as a sheet of *nori* seaweed. (Here a sheet of cooked egg is substituted.) Those called *chirashi zushi* consist of rice filled or topped with bits or slices of various vegetables and seafood, arranged in a lacquer box. There are other kinds of Sushi, but these are the main types.

With the following recipe you can make at one time examples of all three kinds.

In Japan (and some large American cities), Sushi not only is made at home but at shops or stands which far surpass a hot dog or hamburger stand in appearance. All the colorful ingredients are attractively displayed in an attractive setting, one element of which may be a slanting wood bar behind which customers sit and direct the Sushi-maker to prepare just what they happen to crave at the moment.

This recipe is a good introduction to Sushi. You do not have to face such jarring experiences as eating seaweed, raw fish, octopus, eel, or dried gourd—ingredients often encountered. Everything is quite ordinary—yet authentic. Later you can graduate to more exotic Sushi.

Serve Japanese soup or salad and these three kinds of Sushi and you have a whole meal for 4 to 6 people.

To make the three kinds, you proceed this way: First you prepare the seasoned rice mixture (enough for all) and some ingredients to incorporate. Then you follow shaping instructions for each kind—**Rolled Sushi, Sushi with Prawns, and Sushi with Vegetable Tidbits.**

4 cups short-grain rice (description on page 8)
  Water
  Sugar
  White vinegar or white rice vinegar (description on page 10)
  Salt
2 ounces large dried mushrooms (description on page 16)
  Soy sauce
2 large carrots
4 to 5 oz. small cooked shrimp (canned if you like)
  Red food coloring
6 eggs
2 tablespoons chicken broth, water, or white rice wine (sake, description on page 10)
4 large green beans, or 6 long strands of watercress
12 large, raw, unshelled shrimp
  Wasabi Paste or hot mustard, optional (directions with Sashimi recipe on page 70)
  Pickled red ginger, optional (description on page 11)
1 package (10 oz.) frozen green peas

The Rice Mixture (Sushi Meshi): Put 4 cups short-grain rice into a large, heavy pan. Add 4 cups cold water and 4 teaspoons sugar; soak about 2 hours. Cover and bring to a boil on high heat until the water begins to spew out from the lid. Without lifting the lid, turn heat immediately to low (on an electric range, have one of the units preheated to low and immediately transfer the pan of rice). Cook for 12 minutes on low heat; remove from heat and let stand 10 minutes, all without lifting the lid.

Meanwhile, combine in a small pan ½ cup white vinegar, 6 tablespoons sugar, and 4 teaspoons salt; heat just until sugar is dissolved.

Also have ready an electric hair dryer or have someone standing by who can fan the rice mixture to cool it quickly as you add the vinegar mixture (this prevents the rice from becoming soggy). Turn the cooked rice immediately into a large bowl and carefully fold in the vinegar mixture while fanning or cooling it with the hair dryer set on "cool," being careful to keep the rice grains whole.

Mushroom Strips: Soak mushrooms in water to cover for 30 minutes to 1 hour. Rinse, drain, and cut into long, thin strips, discarding stems. Put sliced mushrooms into a small pan with 2 tablespoons *each* sugar, soy sauce, water, and 1 teaspoon salt. Cover pan and simmer until the water is evaporated and mushrooms are tender, about 5 minutes. *(Continued on page 86)*

SOME IMPORTANT STEPS IN MAKING SUSHI

ROLLED SUSHI with Egg Wrapper is made by topping wrapper on mat with rice and strip of filling.

NEXT, MAT is rolled and pressed to form a firm roll. (See Three Kinds of Sushi recipe opposite.)

FINISHED ROLLED SUSHI is sliced crosswise into pieces easy to pick up; filling is in the center.

SUSHI WITH PRAWNS (Three Kinds of Sushi) is made by pressing rice onto butterflied shrimp.

Carrot Strips: Cut carrots into long, thin strips. Put into a small pan with 2 teaspoons white vinegar, 2 tablespoons sugar, ¾ teaspoon salt, and 1½ tablespoons water. Cover pan and simmer until tender-crisp and until the liquid is evaporated, about 5 minutes.

Pink Shrimp: Combine small, cooked shrimp with 1 tablespoon sugar; add a couple of drops of red food coloring, blended with 1 teaspoon water. Grind the shrimp mixture until shrimp is flaky and color evenly distributed. Do this by stirring and pressing in a wire strainer, or use the mortar and pestle *(suribachi)* sketched on page 20.

Put into a small pan and stir over low heat until shrimp is dry and fluffy.

Egg Pancakes: You will need a square frying pan measuring 8 to 10 inches (an electric frying pan works well) and a wide pancake turner or two. Combine the 6 eggs, 3 tablespoons sugar, ¾ teaspoon salt, and the 2 tablespoons chicken broth, water, or wine; beat with a wire whip or fork until well blended and the sugar is dissolved.

Preheat the frying pan to medium low (about 250°), grease it well, pour in ⅓ to ½ cup of egg mixture, and quickly tip and tilt pan to coat bottom evenly. When the egg is slightly browned, carefully turn to cook other side (if it should tear, patch it with a little of the egg mixture). When done, remove it to a piece of paper towel to absorb any excess grease. Make a total of 3 pancakes.

Green Vegetable: Cook 4 green beans until tender in boiling, salted water, then cut in long, thin strips. Or drop watercress into boiling water until bright green and limp.

Rolled Sushi with Egg Wrapper. You can use a bamboo place mat or the kind made especially for Sushi *(sudare)* sketched on page 20.

Place the mat with strands parallel to you. Place an egg pancake on the mat. Have a bowl of cold water beside you for moistening your hands as you work with the rice.

Put about 1½ cups of the rice mixture on the egg pancake; with moist hands, pat down to about ½ inch thickness, spreading rice to edges of egg on both sides and the bottom edge, and to within about 2 inches of top. *See photographs on preceding page.*

In the middle of the rice arrange a horizontal row of a third of the cooked mushroom strips, and a row of a third of the cooked carrot strips. With a small spoon, sprinkle a row of a third of

the pink shrimp over carrots and mushrooms. Also arrange a row of the green vegetable, either green beans or watercress.

Holding the center ingredients down with fingers, lift up mat with thumbs and roll over until the near edge of the wrapper meets the far edge of the *rice* (not the far edge of wrapper). Pull mat away as you roll the egg and rice—use a little pressure to tighten roll. Press in any loose ingredients at ends of the roll.

Wrap in waxed paper or clear plastic film and chill at least an hour before slicing. Repeat, making 1 more roll. (Save one egg pancake and a third *each* of the mushrooms, carrots, and pink shrimp for Sushi with Vegetable Tidbits.)

When rolls are chilled, use a sharp, moistened knife to cut into about 1½-inch-thick slices. Makes 12 Sushi slices.

Sushi with Prawns. Run a bamboo skewer lengthwise through each unshelled large, raw shrimp (prawn), to keep it from curling as it cooks.

Drop the shrimp into boiling, salted water and cook about 5 minutes; cool. Remove the skewers and shell and devein, leaving on tails. Butterfly each by slitting lengthwise on *underside* almost to the back.

Marinate the shrimp in a mixture of ½ cup white vinegar, 2 tablespoons sugar, and ½ teaspoon salt for about 30 minutes. Drain and lay them flat on a plate. Dab a very small amount of Wasabi Paste or hot mustard inside each shrimp, if you wish.

With moistened hands, take up a little of the rice mixture (about size of a walnut) and press into each split shrimp. *(See photograph on preceding page.)* Decorate each with a strip of pickled red ginger, if available. Or serve the ginger, thinly sliced, on the side. You might also serve these Sushi with a small cup of soy sauce for dipping. Makes 12 Sushi.

Sushi with Vegetable Tidbits. Cook frozen peas in salted water as directed on the package; drain. Put the remainder of the rice mixture (after making other two kinds of Sushi) in a bowl with the drained peas; cut the remaining mushroom strips and carrot strips into small pieces and add to rice. Mix all together carefully so you do not mash the rice grains.

Turn into a serving dish, which might be a plastic container, square or rectangular pan, bowl, or lacquer tray or box. (If possible, make individual servings rather than one large one.)

Cut the remaining egg pancake into very thin strips. Arrange the egg strips and the remaining pink shrimp on top. Makes 4 to 6 servings.

DESSERTS, SWEETS & BEVERAGES

All the Oriental cuisines are favored by calorie-conscious Americans for several reasons, one being their low fat content and another being the pleasant custom of no dessert. If the Chinese have few sweets, perhaps the Japanese have even fewer. Such foods are usually snacks or tea delicacies.

Lima Bean Kinton

Desserts are not traditional with Japanese meals, originally because sugar was in short supply and now partially because so many dishes contain a little sweetness and the sweet tooth is satisfied along the way.

However, some tea-time pastries and confections are often served by restaurants in America who must offer desserts to customers accustomed to such. Many of these confections are made from sweetened beans—red or black ones, or lima beans. The recipe following is for one kind you can make at home easily.

This obviously is a dessert to serve to the adventuresome only. It also might be wise to offer an alternate dessert from those suggested in Desserts You Can Buy in the next column.

  1 **can (1 lb.) lima beans, undrained**
  ¼ **teaspoon salt**
  ½ **cup sugar**
      Green food coloring

Remove skins from lima beans and mash beans. (Or press beans through a coarse wire strainer to remove skins.) Place bean pulp and liquid, salt, and sugar in a small saucepan. Stirring often, cook over medium heat until mixture forms a ball and begins to pull away from sides of pan, about 20 minutes. Cool.

Force mixture through a wire strainer or food mill. Mix in enough coloring to make a bright green. Roll mixture into 12 small balls. Let dry uncovered at room temperature for 1 to 2 hours. Then wrap loosely in plastic film and refrigerate until serving time if desired. Each serving may be threaded on bamboo skewers, then placed on a small plate. Makes 6 servings.

Desserts You Can Buy

Desserts are not usually served with Japanese meals, although in the big cities now French pastries and other foreign delicacies are becoming popular.

Nevertheless, there are at least four different kinds of things you can serve at the end of a meal which will be compatible with the food—fruit, tea pastries, sweet or savory crackers (some much like cookies), and certain wines or liqueurs.

Fruit. Either fresh or canned fruit is probably the nicest and most appreciated finale because it is mildly sweet and light. The Japanese love melon and select strawberries beautifully presented. You could serve these, or any other fresh fruits, on a bed of cracked ice. A whole orange or tangerine on a little dish, garnished with a leaf, would be typical.

Several special Japanese fruits are available canned, at Japanese and some gourmet stores. White ("snow") peaches and pears called *nizyu-seiki* come in syrup. A special mixture of fruits called *Mitsumame* also is canned. This contains peaches, cherries, oranges, apples, and two unusual ingredients—little cubes of gelatin made from *kanten* (agar-agar) and small red beans.

A few preserved kumquats or a piece of ginger preserved in syrup can give a piquant lift to the palate (the English people have taken to these two as a replacement for dessert). A recipe for preserving kumquats is on page 66.

Tea Pastries. Most Americans don't like most Japanese tea specialties, which you can buy at Japanese shops.

But a few of these can be pleasing, such as *Yokan*, a gelatinous block of sweetened bean paste, sometimes flavored with chestnuts or persimmons. Packaged Yokan keeps indefinitely without refrigeration. Serve each person just one or two thin slices.

Crackers. The Japanese make an infinite variety of crispy small crackers or cookies from both rice and wheat flour. *Sembei* and *arare* are general names for them. The Chinese fortune cooky is a variety of these, which many authorities claim originated in Japan.

One of the tastiest of the sweet types is coated with ginger-flavored sugar and called *Shoga (ginger) Sembei*. These are sold in cellophane bags in many stores. Another readily likeable type is Peanut *Maki*, a sesame-studded crisp cracker, wrapped around a whole peanut.

Many sembei and arare are not sweet, but salty and savory with soy sauce, sesame, seaweed, and many other flavorings. These are made in many different shapes and legends are told about how each shape came to be invented. These are sold in cellophane bags, boxes, or tins. Read the list of ingredients (required by law) to decide whether you might like the flavor.

Wines and Liqueurs. Rather than dessert, you might decide that a sweet wine is just the proper ending. The Japanese make at least three kinds you may be able to buy—plum, cherry blossom (cherry), and honey apple. They also make liqueur from green tea, which you may or may not like.

Sweet sherry, sweet vermouth, fruit-flavored brandy, and fruit or mint-flavored liqueurs also would be compatible with the foods.

How to Brew Green Tea

Japanese usually drink green tea, and the black tea sold is regarded as foreign. Actually, both types come from the same plant and are just processed differently. Leaves are merely dried for green tea; they are fermented to make the black type.

Green tea comes in many grades from the very coarse and cheap *bancha* to delicate and expensive *gyokuro*. These are brewed differently. Briskly boiling water is poured over *bancha* and the coarser teas, but the water is cooled somewhat before being poured on the better grades. The better the tea, the more the water is cooled.

Green tea should not be brewed too strong or it becomes bitterish and loses its fragrance. About 1 scant teaspoon of leaves per cup of water is sufficient. You may even find that less is desirable if you brew a large pot. Let the tea steep at least 3 minutes before serving.

There are several interesting variations to green tea. One is labelled *roasted* green tea; the leaves are brownish and impart a roasted flavor. Another called *genmai cha* ("cha" means tea) contains toasted glutinous rice, some grains of which have exploded and look like little popcorn. The rice, mixed right in with the tea leaves, gives the beverage a sweet and nutty flavor. A powdered tea called *matcha* is used for the famous Japanese tea ceremony.

All the teas mentioned here are available in Japanese stores. Green tea of fine quality but unlabelled as to Japanese type is sold at some supermarkets and gourmet shops.

Green tea is always drunk plain, with no sugar or anything else added.

How to Serve Sake

The faintly sweet Japanese white rice wine, *sake*, is served warm with meals, poured from a sake jug into tiny cups. Jugs and cups are sketched on page 21. (The jugs can double as sauce, syrup, or melted-butter servers for American meals; the cups can also be used for after-dinner liqueurs.)

Most large liquor stores carry sake, which closely resembles dry vermouth in flavor.

To Heat Sake. Place either the opened bottle or filled sake jug in a pan of water. The water should come up on the outside to about where the sake is. Heat the water just until it begins to simmer; turn off heat and let sit several minutes. Dry bottle or jug before taking to the table.

A KOREAN RECIPE SAMPLER

Some dishes popular with those who visit Korea

Korean cooking bears some resemblance to Chinese cooking, some resemblance to Japanese, and at the same time is different from either.

A particular Korean dish may remind you of a dish from one or both of the other two countries. Nevertheless, almost always it will have its own distinctive Korean flavor, appearance, and aroma.

The fact that Korea is a northern country has shaped its cuisine. The food tends to be hearty, richly seasoned, and rib-sticking. Ingredients are those available in more northern areas.

Several seasonings (used in all Oriental cooking) predominate and are responsible for the food's individuality. These are red pepper (chiles), sesame seed, and sesame oil. Much Korean food is nippy or even quite hot with pepper and has a rich, nutty aroma of sesame and its flavorful oil.

Korean food cannot be discussed without mentioning Kim Chee, fermented vegetable pickles, which are served with most meals and even cooked into many dishes. Few foreigners who have been to Korea are neutral about Kim Chee and its odor in particular. They love it or hate it.

A recipe for Kim Chee made of cabbage (the most popular vegetable) is on page 92.

Another food that appears on the table almost as often as Kim Chee is called simply Kim. This is toasted laver seaweed, which is eaten like a cracker or crumbled over the food.

Other characteristics of Korean food have to do with the frequency with which certain common ingredients or types of foods are used. Beef, for example, is not often eaten in southern China and Japan where it is very expensive. But in Korea beef is an important meat.

Plain rice is eaten in Korea, just as in the other Oriental countries. But often rice is cooked with other things such as potatoes, beans, mushrooms, bean sprouts, and chestnuts. Chinese and Japanese cooks may sometimes add such things to rice. But Korean cooks prepare these rice combinations often.

Beef Barbecue Appetizers

This hot appetizer takes only two minutes to cook, whether you barbecue it over charcoal or cook it in a frying pan. Use a very narrow grill or cake rack over the barbecue coals so the meat strips will not fall through.

Or use the special Genghis Khan grill pictured on page 93 and described on page 22.

The Korean Banquet menu features this dish on page 27.

> 1 pound chuck roast, cut 1½ to 2-inches thick
> 2 tablespoons salad oil or sesame oil
> ¼ cup soy sauce
> 1 teaspoon garlic powder
> 1½ teaspoons vinegar
> Pepper
> 1½ teaspoons crushed toasted sesame seed
> (see recipe at bottom of page 93)
> ¼ teaspoon cayenne (or less if desired)
> 1 green onion and top, sliced

Cut meat across the grain in very thin slices. If slices are longer than 3 inches, cut them in half. Place meat in a bowl with the oil, soy sauce, garlic powder, vinegar, a sprinkling of pepper, crushed sesame seed, cayenne, and onion. Mix with your hands until well blended. Cover and chill in refrigerator for at least 4 hours.

To cook, place meat strips on a rack over charcoal and barbecue for 1 minute on each side. Meat should be brown but not crusty. Or, if you wish, heat a large frying pan, toss in meat, and cook over high heat for 2 minutes, stirring occasionally. Provide bamboo skewers or toothpicks for spearing the meat. Serves 4 to 6.

Sin Sul Lo

This dish, always reserved for special occasions in Korea, is historically an even more elaborate creation than the relatively simplified version here.

The foods are partially cooked ahead and concisely arranged, in the kitchen, in the cooking pot. The pot is then brought to the table where broth is poured in and the cooking finished.

The vessel traditionally used is the charcoal-fired "hot pot," but other utensils such as an electric frying pan can be used. For complete details, see the section on Cook-at-the-Table equipment on page 19.

A menu featuring the dish is on page 29.

¼ **cup sesame seed**
¼ **cup soy sauce**
½ **clove garlic, minced or mashed**
2 **tablespoons salad oil**
1 **pound lean, tender beef such as sirloin or tenderloin, thinly sliced**
1 **pound ground pork**
  About 45 pine nuts, pistachio nuts, or pieces of walnut
  Cornstarch
2 **eggs, slightly beaten**
  Salad oil for frying
1 **pound spinach**
¼ **pound fresh mushrooms**
2 **medium-sized turnips, peeled**
2 **medium-sized carrots, peeled**
  Boiling, salted water
  Garnishes (suggestions follow)
8 **cups regular-strength beef broth**

Toast the sesame seed by stirring them in a dry pan over medium heat until browned; combine with soy sauce, garlic, and 2 tablespoons salad oil.

Cut the beef slices into 2 or 3-inch wide strips (width of the moat in the "hot pot"); marinate for 1 to 2 hours in half of the sesame-soy mixture.

Combine the remaining sesame-soy mixture with the ground pork; form small balls, inserting a nut meat in the middle of each. Roll balls in cornstarch to lightly coat them, then dip in the beaten egg. Lightly brown the pork balls on all sides in a frying pan with a small amount of the salad oil.

Remove stems from the spinach; blanch leaves in boiling water just until limp. Carefully place leaves to make stacks about ½-inch deep; dip in cornstarch, coating the stacks all over, then dip in beaten egg. Sauté the spinach stacks in salad oil until lightly browned, then cut each into slices about 1½ inches wide.

Slice the mushrooms and sauté lightly in salad oil. Cook the turnips and carrots in boiling, salted water just until tender. Thinly slice the turnips and cut to fit the width of the moat if the "hot pot" is used. Score the carrots length-wise about ¼-inch deep on 4 sides, then cut in thin slices—each slice should resemble a flower blossom.

Arrange a section of half of each ingredient clockwise in the cooker in this order: turnips, marinated beef, carrots, mushrooms, spinach slices, and meat balls. Repeat until cooker is filled.

Arrange your choice of garnishes alternately on top.

Set the cooking pot in the middle of the table. Pour in the beef broth, which has been reheated in the kitchen. Cover the cooker and allow to simmer for several minutes, then remove the cover. Let guests help themselves from the common pot, using chopsticks or forks. After all foods have been eaten, ladle broth into soup bowls for sipping. Serves 4 to 6.

Garnishes. Use a small amount of several of these: slices of hard-cooked eggs, green onion tops, pine nuts, blanched walnuts, sliced steamed fish cakes called *kamaboko* (see page 12 for description), or mushroom slices, spinach slices, or pork balls saved from the cooking ingredients.

Korean Dumpling Soup

Korean *mandoo* (meat-filled dumplings) are similar to Chinese *won ton*. Generally, Korean cooks simmer a chicken to make the soup broth. Then they cut the meat into neat sections and season it with soy sauce, toasted sesame seed, garlic, pepper, and onions and serve it as a side dish. In this adaptation just canned chicken broth is used.

The Korean Banquet menu features this dish on page 27.

  1 cup fresh or canned bean sprouts (description on page 14)
 ¼ head of a small regular white cabbage
  1 fresh soy bean cake 2½-inches square (dow foo or tofu, description on page 14); or 1 egg, slightly beaten
  1 tablespoon salad oil
 ¼ pound chuck roast or round steak, chopped
  3 green onions and tops, chopped
1½ tablespoons soy sauce
1½ teaspoons crushed toasted sesame seed (recipe at bottom of page 93)
60 won ton noodles (3-inches square), purchased or made from recipe on page 62
  2 cans (48 oz. each) regular-strength chicken broth
     Chopped green onions and tops for garnish

Cook fresh bean sprouts in boiling water 3 minutes; drain and chop. (Canned sprouts do not need to be cooked.) Cook cabbage in boiling water 5 minutes; drain, chop. Drain bean cake.

Heat salad oil in a frying pan, then brown meat quickly with 1 of the chopped green onions; add soy sauce and simmer 2 minutes.

Place bean sprouts, cabbage, soy bean cake (or beaten egg), meat mixture, and the remainder of the chopped green onion in a bowl; add ½ teaspoon of the crushed sesame seed. Mash together until soy bean cake loses its identity.

Place 1 teaspoon filling in the center of each won ton noodle square; dampen edges slightly, then fold in half diagonally like a turnover to form a dumpling. Pinch edges together to seal. Cover filled dumplings with plastic wrap and refrigerate until ready to use. (Do not fill dumplings more than 4 hours before cooking.)

To cook, heat chicken broth with the remaining 1 teaspoon crushed sesame seed: drop dumplings into boiling broth, one at a time. (To keep dumplings from sticking together, cook only 20 at a time.) After they rise to the top, cook for an additional 4 minutes. For each serving, ladle broth and 5 or 6 dumplings into a bowl and sprinkle with onion. Serves 10 to 12.

Watercress Salad

The Korean salad-relish, called *Namul*, may be made with various vegetables. It is usually flavored with such things as green onion, soy sauce, red chiles, and sesame, all found in this recipe.

The Korean Banquet menu features this dish on page 27.

  2 bunches watercress
  2 small green onions and tops, chopped
 ¼ teaspoon pepper
 ¾ teaspoon salt
1½ teaspoons sugar
  2 tablespoons soy sauce
1½ tablespoons vinegar
  1 dried red chile (about 1-inch long), crushed
  1 teaspoon crushed toasted sesame seed (recipe at bottom of page 93)

Wash watercress; drain, then cut into 2-inch lengths. Mix together the green onions and tops, pepper, salt, sugar, soy sauce, vinegar, and crushed chile. Pour over watercress, then sprinkle with sesame seed. Chill for 1 hour, if you like, but serve at room temperature. Serves 4.

If you prefer a milder dressing, let the whole chile stand in the dressing for 1 hour and remove it before dressing the greens.

Rice & Bean Sprouts

Team this with the Short Rib Barbecue on page 93 for a simple meal.

  3 tablespoons crushed toasted sesame seed (recipe at bottom of page 93)
  2 minced green onions
  1 clove garlic, minced or mashed
  1 tablespoon salad oil or sesame oil
1½ cups bean sprouts
  2 cups hot cooked rice
  2 tablespoons soy sauce

Combine sesame seed with onions and garlic and sauté in the oil for 3 minutes. Add the bean sprouts and sauté until thoroughly hot. (It may be necessary to add a few drops of water to keep ingredients from sticking.) Add the hot rice and soy sauce and gently mix, being careful not to mash rice grains. Serves 4 to 6.

Braised Chicken

Dried mushrooms and soy sauce give a rich, dark color to the sauce for this chicken. Korean cooks seldom make a gravy out of a sauce, but you may prefer to thicken it slightly with cornstarch.

The Korean Banquet menu features this dish on page 27.

    4 ounces dried mushrooms (description
          on page 16)
    3 tablespoons soy sauce
    1 tablespoon salad oil
    2 cloves garlic, mashed or minced
    ½ teaspoon pepper
    1 large broiler-fryer chicken (2½ to 3 lbs.),
          cut in small (2-inch) pieces if possible
    2 tablespoons salad oil
    1 large onion, cut in 8 wedges
    2 stalks celery, cut diagonally in 1-inch lengths
    ½ cup toasted slivered almonds
    4 green onions and tops, cut in 1-inch lengths

Wash mushrooms well and cover with cold water; let stand overnight. Combine the soy sauce, the 1 tablespoon salad oil, garlic, and pepper; marinate chicken in sauce 30 minutes.

Heat the 2 tablespoons salad oil in a frying pan; remove chicken from marinade, drain well, and brown slowly. Cut the mushrooms in strips ¼-inch wide, removing stems. Then add to the browned chicken along with ½ cup of the mushroom liquid, onion, celery, and the remaining marinade. Cover and simmer until chicken is tender, about 40 minutes. Garnish with almonds and green onions. Serves 4.

Cabbage Pickles

Kim Chee is featured in the Korean Banquet menu on page 27.

    1 large head celery cabbage (description on
          page 15, or one small head regular
          white cabbage
       Salt
    4 green onions and tops
    1 large clove garlic, minced
    1 dried hot red chile (about 2-inches long),
          crushed
    1 teaspoon grated fresh ginger root

Cut cabbage in pieces 1-inch long and 1-inch wide. Sprinkle 2 tablespoons salt on, mix well, and let stand 15 minutes.

Cut green onions and tops in 1½-inch lengths, then cut lengthwise in thin slices. Wash salted cabbage three times with cold water; add the onions, garlic, chile, ginger, 1 tablespoon salt, and enough water to cover; mix well. Cover and let stand for a few days.

Taste mixture every day. When it is acid enough, cover and refrigerate up to 2 weeks. Makes about 1 quart.

(Note: You can buy Kim Chee also—in bottles at Oriental and gourmet stores.)

Skewered Beef & Mushrooms

For this dish, called *Sanjuck,* you thread beef strips, mushrooms, and green onions on skewers. Then you dip them in flour and egg, and fry.

The Korean Banquet menu on page 27 features this dish.

    ½ pound beef top round, cut ⅜-inch thick
    1 can (3 or 4 oz.) sliced mushrooms, drained
    2 tablespoons each salad oil or sesame oil,
          and soy sauce
    1 teaspoon crushed toasted sesame seed
          (recipe on opposite page)
    1 clove garlic, mashed or minced
    ½ teaspoon sugar
       Pepper
    2 bunches green onions
       Flour
    3 eggs, well beaten
       Salad oil for frying

Cut meat across the grain in strips ¼-inch thick, then cut in 2-inch lengths. Toss meat in a bowl with the drained mushrooms, oil, soy sauce, crushed sesame seed, garlic, sugar, and a dash of pepper; mix lightly and let stand at least 15 minutes. Trim and wash onions; cut in 2-inch lengths, cutting only to where tops separate.

On short skewers thread 2 pieces of meat (fold strips in half if they are too long), then 2 pieces of onion (skewer crosswise), then 2 mushroom slices; repeat with another 2 pieces of meat, 2 onions, and 2 mushrooms. Roll skewers in flour, then in beaten eggs; let stand 5 minutes.

Cover bottom of frying pan with salad oil, and heat until medium-hot; place skewers in pan and cook until golden brown and crusty, about 10 minutes on each side.

If you fry these early in the day, reheat in a 375° oven for 10 minutes before serving. Serves 4.

SHORT RIB BARBECUE (recipe below), scored for appearance and quick cooking, is broiled over charcoal on domed Genghis Khan grill. A regular hibachi or other barbecue can be used.

Short Rib Barbecue

A special way of cutting short ribs distinguishes this dish. When you buy the short ribs, ask your meat man to saw through the bone at 2½-inch intervals so you can dice-cut meat chunks as described.

To broil, use a regular barbecue or hibachi, or the domed Genghis Khan grill which lets the fat drain off without catching fire, *pictured in the photo above.*

- 4 pounds well-trimmed beef short ribs, sawed through bone
- ½ cup each soy sauce and water
- ¼ cup sliced green onions with tops
- 2 tablespoons sesame seed
- 2 2 tablespoons sugar
- 2 cloves garlic, minced or mashed
- ½ teaspoon pepper

Cut short ribs into approximately 2½-inch cubes. With bone side down, dice-cut this way: Cut cubes halfway to bone every ½ inch in one direction; at right angles, cut every ½ inch, but go only ½ inch deep. Combine remaining ingredients to make marinade. Put scored pieces of meat into marinade and chill, covered, in refrigerator for 4 to 5 hours.

Place meat, bone side down, on barbecue grill over high heat. When brown, turn and cook on meat side. Lift and turn meat throughout cooking time (about 15 minutes) to expose all surfaces to the heat. Cook until crisply browned. Provide plenty of napkins so the meat can be eaten out of hand. Makes 4 main-dish servings, or 10 to 12 appetizer servings.

Crushed Toasted Sesame Seed

In many of the Korean recipes you use crushed toasted sesame seed prepared this way: Place sesame seed in a heavy frying pan. Stirring, cook over medium heat 10 minutes·or until golden brown. Turn seed into a mortar, add 1 teaspoon salt for each 1 cup seed and crush with a pestle. Or crush by whirling in an electric blender. Store in a tightly covered jar.

Index